The Taotie Image in
Chinese Art, Culture, and Cosmology™

中國文化藝術及宇宙論中的饕餮紋

Dave Alber

CHINESE TRANSLATION
BY AN ANONYMOUS FRIEND

What are reviewers saying about Dave's books?

"As someone who is passionately committed to the survival of both the world's treasure trove of myths and the indigenous peoples who conjured up so many of those marvelous stories, I deeply admire Dave Alber's anthology, *The Heart of Myth*. This collection of wisdom stories is the book lover's equivalent of spinning a globe and vowing to travel wherever your finger lands, and to learn and respect the traditions you find there."

Phil Cousineau
Author of *Once and Future Myths*, *The Art of Pilgrimage*, and host of *Global Spirit* on LINK TV

"Alber's work is grounded in the notion of myth-making itself. The personal and the interpersonal mix and mesh, to become something new, something that breaks the static desires of culture itself."

Maggie Macary, Ph.D.
Creator of *Myth & Culture*

"*Alien Sex in Silicon Valley* takes the reader into a most remarkable experience! The reader will find herself or himself taken into a story about being taken into a story. ... Importantly provocative!"

David L. Miller, Ph.D.
Watson-Ledden Professor of Religion, Emeritus, Syracuse University
Author of *Three Faces of God*, *Hells and Holy Ghosts*, and *Gods and Games*

"Dave Alber's *To the Dawn* is a tour de force in dramatic, robust poetry."

Dennis Patrick Slattery, Ph.D.
Author of *Casting the Shadows: Selected Poems* and *Just Below the Water Line*

ISBN-10: 1497355206
ISBN-13: 978-1497355200

DEDICATION

This book is respectfully dedicated to
everyone who loves and appreciates
ancient Chinese culture.
Dave Alber, MA

僅以此書奉獻給
所有熱愛與欣賞中國古代文化的讀者。
Dave Alber, MA

CONTENTS

ACKNOWLEDGMENTS

In 2009, I had the good fortune of attending Liu Ming's *Yin Earth Ox Year* talk at U.C. Berkeley in California. As a prelude to his lecture, he spoke about Chinese Taoism's cultural indebtedness to the tradition of Siberian Shamanism. I was quite struck by his comments, because when I think of Siberian Shamanism, I immediately reflect on how the tradition is one of the most intact living communities that still reflects the life-ways of Paleolithic Pan-Eurasian reindeer hunting traditions (80,000 BCE to 7,000 BCE in Asia.) This makes it one of the oldest living religious systems and cosmologies on the planet. And to hear of its continuity though Taoism and other Asian traditions struck me as quite profound. The book *Bo & Bon* by Dmitry Ermakov reaffirmed Liu Ming's perspective and added to my own understanding of this great, though often unacknowledged, tradition. My own background in Mythological Studies, Asian religious systems, and extensive travel in China, Taiwan, India, Nepal, and Thailand helped pull together a picture of Pan-Asian cosmology that could be communicated by tracing this Pan-Asian symbol through Chinese history. My travels also helped in providing the photographic content for this lecture.

This book would not be possible without the help of the many who assisted me in putting the lecture together at Henan Polytechnic University (HPU). I am indebted to the administration and staff of this fine university. I am grateful for Celine (LingLing, Lee), Li Kang, Zhijie Zhang (Angelica), Bill Williams, Laketta Bolton, Nathan Suchomel, Trevor Howell, and all my friends for moral support.

Dave Alber, MA

致谢

2009年，我有幸參加了在加州伯克利分校舉行的劉明關於《Yin Earth Ox Year 》的演講，開始演講前，他談及中國的道教文化受到西伯利亞薩滿教的影響。他的評論讓我相當驚訝，因為當我一想到西伯利亞薩滿教，馬上就會想起，這一教派至今仍延續舊石器時代泛歐亞（西元前80000年到西元前7000年的亞洲）遊牧生活方式，他們是最原始的部落。這點讓它成為全球現存的最古老的宗教體系宇宙學之一。雖然我對道教和其他亞洲教派印象深刻，可是聽到他這麼說都不由得相當驚訝。後來， 德米特裏·埃爾馬科夫在他的著作《Bo &Bon》中再次肯定了劉明的觀點，這更加深了我個人對這個偉大、然而常常不被人們所識的教派的瞭解。我個人從事神學和亞洲宗教體系的研究，加上周遊中國、臺灣、印度、尼泊爾和泰國等地的經歷，有助於我將泛亞宇宙學拼成一張可以在中國史上追溯這種泛亞象徵的圖像。我的旅行經歷也有助於為此次演講提供攝影內容。

衷心感謝河南理工大學（HPU）那些幫我整理講稿的人們，有了他們，此書才得以順利進行。我衷心感謝這所如此優秀的大學裏的管理部門和教師。我要感謝席琳（李玲玲）、李康、張芝潔（安吉莉卡）、比爾威廉斯、拉凱塔博爾頓、南森祖霍梅爾、特雷弗· 豪厄爾，還有我所有朋友和支持者。

Dave Alber, MA

INTRODUCTION:
TAN DUN: THE SOUND OF THE FUTURE

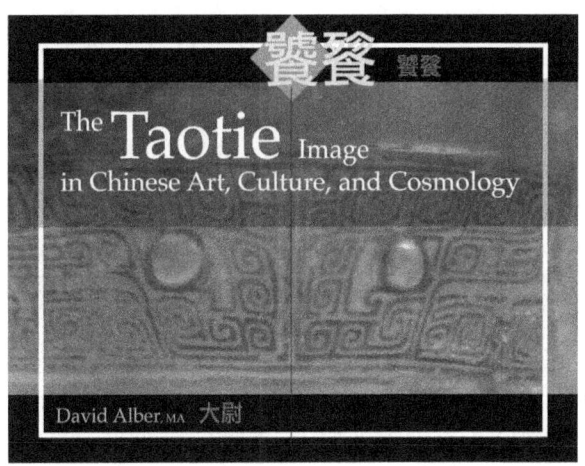

歡迎大家！我是戴夫.阿爾伯。本次演講的主題是中國藝術、文化和宇宙論中的饕餮圖。

Welcome everyone. My name is Dave Alber. And this lecture is on The Taotie Image in Chinese Art, Culture, and Cosmology.

好的，我們從一段音樂開始。在這段首樂中你將聽到殷商時期的編鐘。這是一首現代交響曲，為什麼一首現代音樂交響曲中竟會出現殷商時期的編鐘呢？

［播放音樂］

Okay, so we'll start off with a piece of music. What you'll hear in this musical piece is Shang dynasty bronze bells. And, this is a modern symphony. Why are there Shang dynasty bronze bells in a modern musical symphony?

[Music plays.]

你們剛才聽到的那段音樂是作曲家譚盾所作。你們所有人都聽過這段音樂，因為譚盾是2008年北京奧運會開幕式音樂的作曲者。其實這段音樂，譚盾是為登封少林寺現在播放的那首樂曲而作的，大家都認為這音樂實在太妙了。

The music that you just listened to is by the composer Tan Dun. And you all have heard his music before, because Tan Dun is the composer for the opening ceremonies of the Beijing Olympics in 2008. Actually, Tan Dun did the music for a piece that's playing right now in Dungfung at Shaolin Temple. And it's supposed to be fantastic.

那麼，我們剛才聽到的那段音樂叫《交響曲1996：天地人》，是為了紀念中華人民共和國香港回歸而作的。樂曲的開頭和結尾都有殷商時期的編鐘聲。譚盾在現代交響曲中融入了古代樂器的聲音，我認為這對交響曲來說是非常罕見的。而且在這首樂曲中，你還會聽到兒童合唱的聲音。譚盾在談及此點時說，兒童的歌聲是代表過去，而殷商編鐘的聲音則代表未來。

So, this piece that we just listened to is called *Symphony 1996, Heaven, Earth, Mankind.* This symphony was commissioned to commemorate the reunification of Hong Kong with the People's Republic of China. In the introduction and at the end of the symphony you hear Shang dynasty bronze bells. And I feel that its very unusual for the composer, Tan Dun, to have incorporated the sounds of ancient instruments in a modern composition. In this same piece of music you also hear a children's choir. And so, in talking about this, Tan Dun had said that the voices in the children's choir represent the sound of the past. And the sound of the Shang dynasty bronze bells is the sound of the future.

這是一種非常矛盾的說話，不是嗎？2500年前的殷商編鐘竟然是未來之聲。譚盾的言論裡存在諸多的悖論。我希望在本次演講裡，我們可以一起探討這些悖論。我希望譚盾擺在我們面前的這一悖論能在本次演講裡能起到基本支撐的作用。我希望能以開放概念的形式提出這個悖論。

That's a very paradoxical statement, don't you think? The sound of 2,500-year-old Shang dynasty bronze bells is the sound of the future. There's a lot of paradox in what Tan Dun is saying. And I hope that in this lecture we will be able to explore that paradox. I hope that the paradox that Tan Dun is offering us will serve as a type of sustaining food for us in this lecture. And therefore, I hope to offer this paradox as an opening idea.

PART 1:
AN INTRODUCTION TO THE
TAOTIE IMAGE IN CHINESE ART

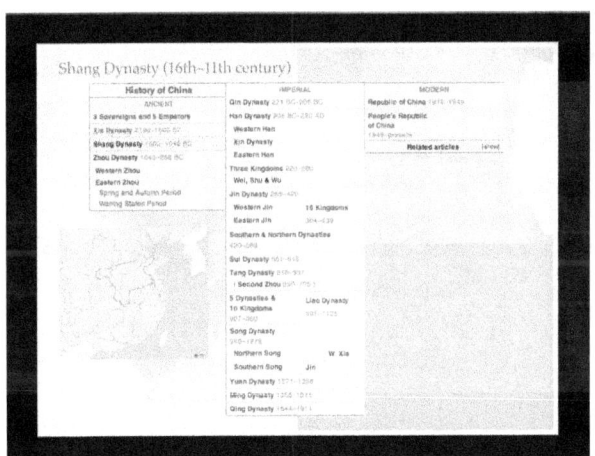

首先讓我們來談談商朝。
Let's talk about the Shang dynasty.

商朝是個遠古朝代，始於西元前十六世紀，止於西元前十七世紀。這裡給大家看看商朝的地理位置，它地理位置位就在這裡的黃河谷。舉例說，商朝舊都就位於今鄭州市附近，殷墟是商朝最後一個首都定址，位於今鄭州安陽稍微向北一帶。如果你去殷墟，走到這條河的對岸，你就能站在當年周軍大敗商軍的地方。

The Shang dynasty is from the sixteenth to the eleventh century BCE. That's a long time ago. Here we show the territory of the Shang dynasty. And this territory was also right here in the Yellow River Valley. The old Shang capital, for example, was our neighboring city Zhengzhou. And the last Shang dynasty capital was a little north of Zhengzhou at Anyang. Yinxu, at Anyang, was the last Shang dynasty capital. And if you go to Yinxu, and go across the river, you can stand where Zhou army stood before they conquered the Shang.

商王朝約興旺了約400多年。因此就這一點而言，商王朝比今天的美國還要古老。商王朝是個統治時間非常長的朝代。

The Shang kingdom flourished for around 400 years. So, to put this into perspective, the Shang kingdom is older than America is today. It's a kingdom that had a very long reign.

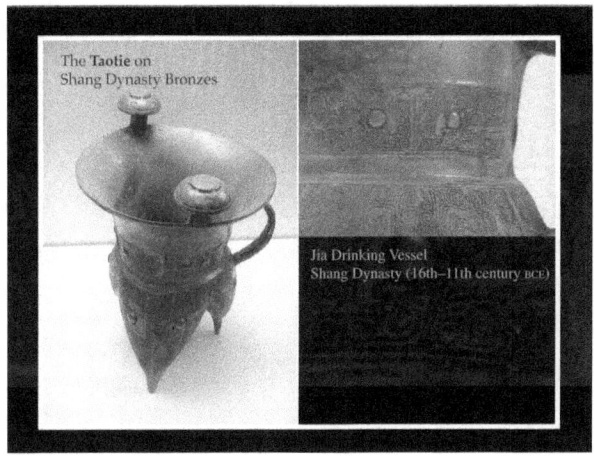

那麼，商朝青銅器上的饕餮紋是什麼呢？這裡我們有個商朝初期（西元前16世紀到西元前11世紀）出產的酒器----斝。這種圖紋就叫饕餮。我們接下來將看到很多這樣的圖案。這種藝術圖紋及象徵是我們本次演講的主題。

Now, what is the taotie on Shang dynasty bronzes? Here we have a Jia drinking vessel that's from the early Shang dynasty, 16th to 11th century BCE. This image is called the taotie. We will see a lot of this image. This art motif and symbol is going to be the topic of this lecture.

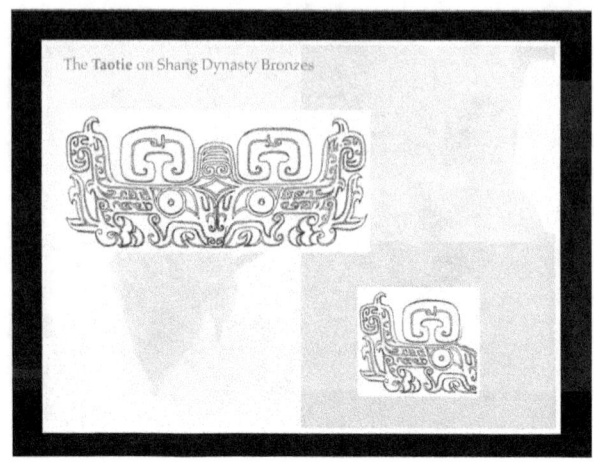

還是這個問題，什麼是饕餮呢？饕餮紋常常被稱作"獸面紋"，因為它看起來像一張野獸的臉----一張掠奪者的臉。我們說這是掠奪者的臉，是因為它的眼長在前額上。以鹿為例，我們發現鹿的眼睛長在頭部的兩側。但是如果我們觀察一隻狼或一隻老虎，會發現這些掠奪者的眼睛長在前面。我們還能看到利牙。犬類的尖牙是用來將肉撕裂。我們還看到利爪。因此，這是一個掠奪者的形象。它的耳朵和尾巴異常警惕，尾巴總是豎直向上。

Again, what is the taotie? The taotie is often called a "beast-mask image", because it looks like the face of a beast. It's a predator face. We can tell it's the face of a predator because it has frontal eyes. If we look at a deer for example, we notice that the deer has eyes on the side of its head. But if we look at a wolf or a tiger, these predators have eyes on the front. And we also see fangs. Canine fangs to tear flesh. We see claws. So, this is the image of a predator. It has very alert ears and a tail. Its tail is always vertical.

饕餮紋一個非常有趣的特色是，如果你將它一分為二，正面圖會變成一個側面。不僅僅是臉部，而是動物全體都這樣。我們能看到嘴、鼻、眼、耳、爪，還有尾部的側面圖。因此，這是一種非常獨特的圖紋，我們能在大多數殷商青銅器上看到這種圖紋。殷商的藝術裡，饕餮紋是非常普遍的。因此，它對商朝人們來說，必定具有非常重要的意義。

A very interesting feature about the taotie image is that if you slice it in half, the frontal image becomes a profile. And not just of the face, but of the whole animal. We see the side view of the mouth, the nose, the eye, the ear, the claws, and then the tail. So, this is a very peculiar image and we see it on most of the Shang dynasty bronzes. It's very prevalent in Shang dynasty art and therefore must have had a lot of importance to the Shang dynasty people.

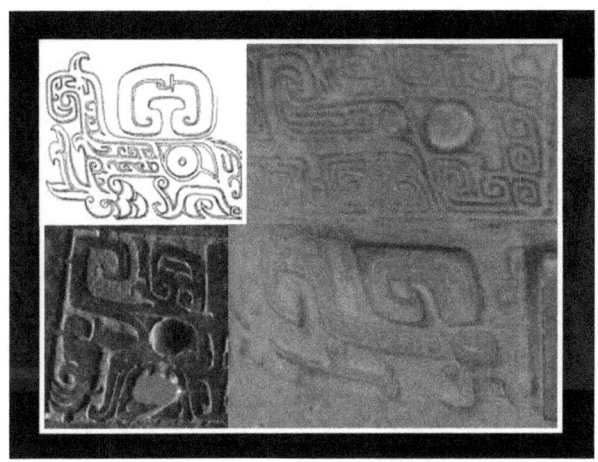

啊，我們這裡有張側面圖。我想給你們展示一些側面圖的樣子。看這邊，它有點程式化，有點像幾何圖形，可是這裡有眼睛，鼻子，耳朵和尾巴。這裡有眼睛、鼻子、耳朵和爪子。我喜歡這尾巴的造型，看起來非常完美。它看上去就像一個狼頭，長著巨大的利牙、警惕的眼睛、銳利的耳朵，還有那鋒利的爪子。

Ah, here we have the side view. I wanted to show the side view in some examples. Here, it's a bit stylized and geometric, but here's the eye, the nose, the ear, and the tail. Here's the eye, the nose, the ear, the claw, and the tail. I like how the tail is done. This one looks perfect. It looks like a wolf's head with huge fangs, an alert eye, and pointed ear, and there's the claw.

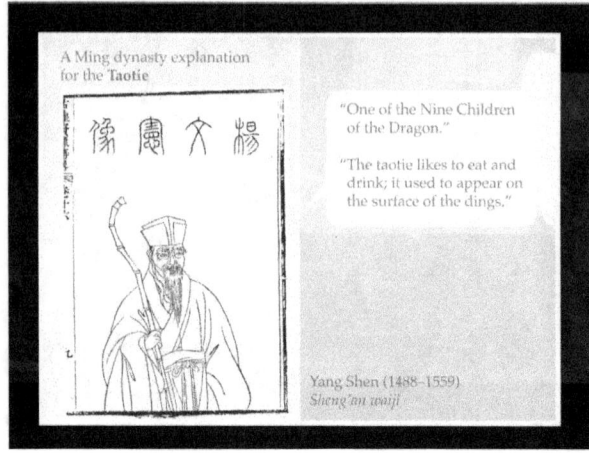

那麼，饕餮紋意味是什麼呢？明朝時期，有個狀元名叫楊慎。他寫了一本關於美學和圖紋藝術的書，書名叫《升庵外集》。楊慎在此書中寫道："饕餮是龍生九子之一，饕餮既貪食又貪喝；它的圖紋經常出現在鼎外。" 因此，從明朝到現今，人們說饕餮紋是一咱勸誡紋，它提醒著人們切不可暴食，它也提醒人們要審慎和自製，飲食或渴求要適度。不過這種對饕餮紋象徵意義的解釋是很後期才出現的。稍後，我們會本次演講裡看到更多的龍之九子。不過楊慎對饕餮象徵意義的解釋也是相當表面的。

So, what does the taotie mean? During the Ming dynasty there was a scholar called Yang Shen. And Yang Shen wrote a book, *Sheng'an waiji*, about aesthetics and art motifs. So, in his book, Yang Shen writes, "The taotie is one of the nine children of the dragon. The taotie likes to eat and drink; it used to appear on the surface of dings." So, from the Ming dynasty up to the present people say that the taotie is a cautionary image. It is a reminder not to be a glutton. It is a reminder to be conservative and to have temperance. It is a reminder to be moderate in our consumption of food or the things that we desire. However, this is a very late explanation for what the taotie means. And we'll see some more of the nine children of the dragon later on in this lecture. Yang Shen's explanation is also a very surface explanation for what the taotie is.

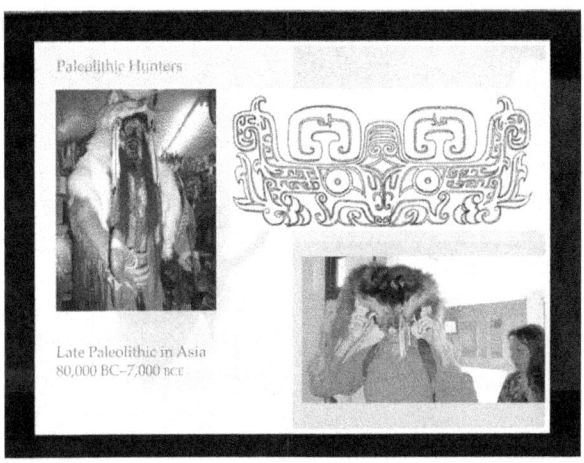

那麼，讓我們再進一步探討這圖紋的象徵意義及其起源。這種圖紋肯定有著非常遠古的起源。亞洲舊石器時代晚期（大約西元前80000年到西元前7000年年）那是很久很久以前的事了。這一時期有人類史上最長的連續文化風格。沒什麼比人類開始在這星球上橫跨歐亞大陸獵殺馴鹿時更久遠的事了。因此，從西元前80000年到西元前7000年，從西班牙到韓國，人類開始獵殺馴鹿。這是一時期持續了很久很久。後來，氣候開始變暖，還有冰山北移。歐亞大陸變暖了，馴鹿開始向北遷移，很多以獵殺馴鹿為生的人也跟著遷移到西伯利亞和歐亞大陸的北部。有的甚至穿越白令海峽去到北美。因此你看到西伯利亞藝術和愛斯基摩藝術，乃至土著印第安人藝術中也有跟饕餮類似的圖紋，特別是那些居住在北美洲大平洋海岸的人們當中。

So, let's go a little deeper into what the image means and where it comes from. What's most likely is that the image has very ancient origins. The late Paleolithic period in Asia was from approximately 80,000 to 7,000 BCE. That's a long time ago. And this is also the longest continuous cultural style in human history. Nothing else can compare to the length of time that human beings on this planet hunted reindeer across Eurasia. So, from 80,000 to 7,000 BCE, from Spain to Korea, human beings hunted reindeer. That's a long time. But eventually, the climate became a lot warmer, and as the ice moved north and as Eurasia became warmer, the reindeer headed north. And so many reindeer hunting people moved into Siberia and northern Eurasia and some of them even crossed the Bering Straight into North America. So, actually you can see images that resemble the taotie in Siberian art and in Eskimo art, and also in the art of Native Americans especially those living on the Pacific coast of North America.

舉例說，殷商青銅器黏土建模技術看起來跟木雕技術很相似。太平洋海岸的北美印第安人的藝術中，很多圖騰柱上面都有跟饕餮類似的圖紋，有的簡直是一模一樣。

For example, the clay modeling technique of Shang dynasty bronzes is made to look like wood carving techniques. And, in the art of the Pacific coast Indians of North America, many totem poles have images which resemble the taotie, some almost in exactitude.

因此我們這裡有個穿獸皮長袍的薩滿圖，他身上的獸皮長袍其實是一塊生剝狼皮。你們看這狼皮是沒有下頜的，因為如果你像當長袍穿的話，剝狼皮時，你必須將下頜去掉。

So, here we have an image of a shaman and he is wearing a flayed animal as a cloak. He's wearing a wolf skin. And you'll see that the wolf skin has no lower jaw because when you skin a wolf you have to remove the lower jaw if you want to wear it as a cloak.

現在我就穿著一塊狼皮，通過狼的眼孔往外看，你看這是狼的爪子，看起來就像饕餮的爪子一樣。所以，饕餮紋很可能是一種起源于舊石器時代的文化風格。

So, here I am wearing a wolf skin. I'm looking through the eyes. Here you get to see the wolf's paws, looking just like the taotie's claws. So, it's very likely that the taotie has its origins in the cultural style of late Paleolithic hunters.

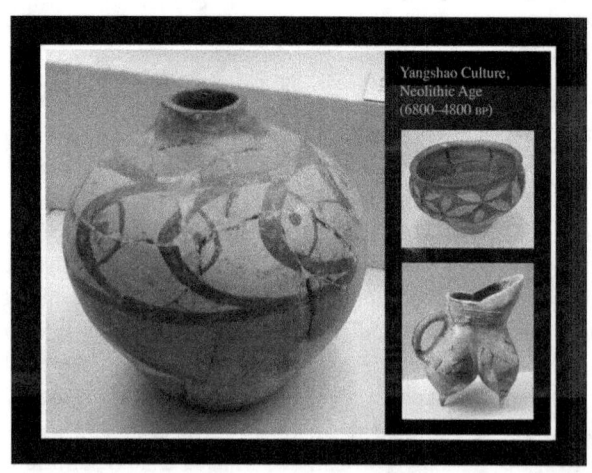

好，現在這裡是西元前6800年到西元前4800年的新石器時代（仰紹文化）。此時期出現了魚、植物、花卉、幾何圖案乃至天文圖形等圖紋，不過那個時期根本就沒有饕餮。這就再次提示饕餮圖紋並不是新石器時代的產物，而是起源於舊石器時代。

So, here we have the Neolithic period, the Yangshao culture from 6800–4800 BP. We have images of fish, plant life, flowers, geometric, and even some astronomical designs, but we don't have the taotie at all. Which again, suggests that the taotie image does not come from the Neolithic but rather that it comes from the Paleolithic.

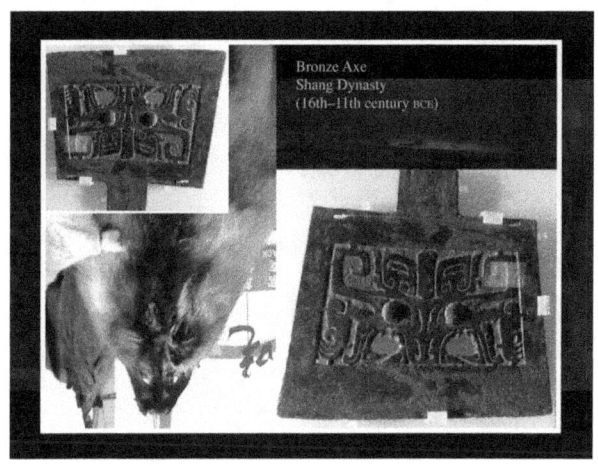

這裡我們有一塊生剝狼皮，旁邊是一把西元前十六世紀到西元前十一世紀的殷商青銅斧。我們看狼皮的圖紋和青銅斧上的圖紋時，會發現它們是如此地相似！我們還看見斧上的圖紋跟一隻被剝了皮的掠食動物極相似。

Here we have a flayed wolf skin next to a bronze ax from the Shang dynasty. This is 16th to 11th century BCE. And we can see when we look at the image of the wolf skin how closely it resembles the image on the bronze ax. We can see that the image on this ax closely resembles a flayed predator animal.

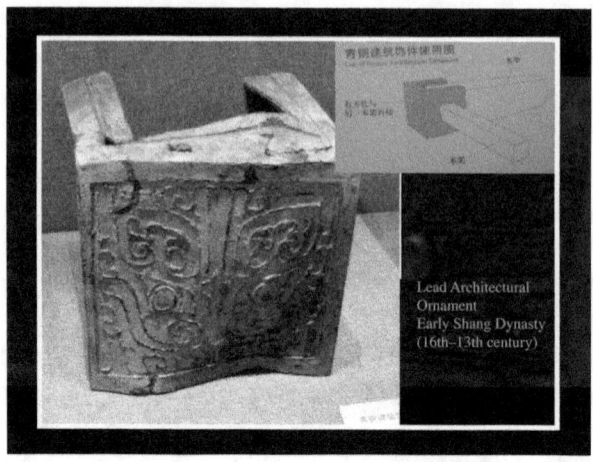

在這張幻燈片裡，我們看到一種建築裝飾的樣式，這是建築物橫樑末端上的裝飾圖紋。這是殷商初期的建築風格，因此是西元前16世紀到西元前13世紀的產物。尤其重要是，直至今天，中國的建築風格仍喜歡採用此類圖紋。因此，殷商初期的建築美學一直沿用到今天。稍後我們將進一步深入探討這種延續性。

On this slide, we have a lead architectural ornament. This ornament was at the end of a beam of a building. This is from the early Shang dynasty, so this was from the 16th to 13th century BCE. What's especially important in this image is that we are still using similar motifs in Chinese architecture up to the present day. So, from the early Shang dynasty we have an aesthetic continuity in architecture that has survived up to the present. We will explore this continuity in depth.

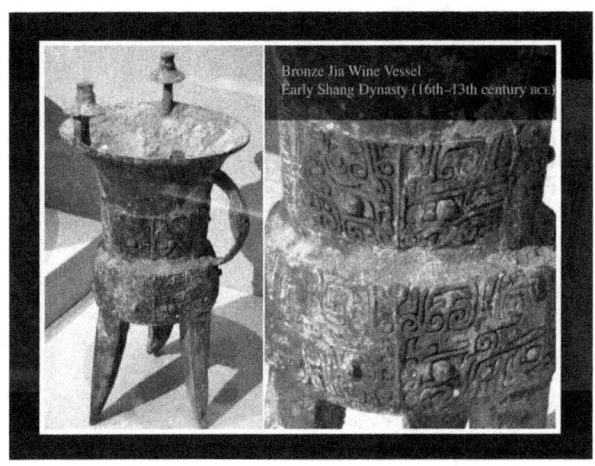

我們這裡有一個酒器----斝。這是殷商初期（西元前十六世紀到西元前十三世紀）的產物。現在，我們看這裡的一幅圖，它的下面還有另一幅圖，我們還看到側邊有更多的圖紋，因此這件青銅器上至少有六到八幅饕餮紋，跟北美土著藝術中繪有跟饕餮相似的動物圖的圖騰柱相比較，不難發現它跟其頂部的圖紋樣式是非常相似的。

Here we have a bronze jia wine vessel. This is early Shang dynasty, from the 16th to 13th century BCE. Now, we see one image here, and one image below it, and we have the suggestion of more images on the side, so this one bronze vessel has at least six or eight taotie images on it. It's easy to compare this image with native North American art where totem poles depict animal images quite similar to the taotie one on top of the other in quite a similar fashion.

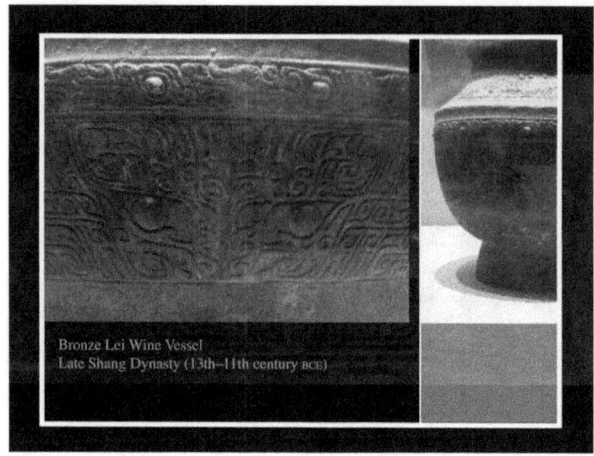

Bronze Lei Wine Vessel
Late Shang Dynasty (13th–11th century BCE)

這裡是個殷商晚期（西元前13世紀到西元前11世紀）的酒器--尊。
這裡我們能看到饕餮紋的側面圖和特寫，這是一種特別漂亮設計。
A bronze lei wine vessel. This is late Shang dynasty, 13th to 11th century
bce. Here we see a view of the side and a close up of the taotie image. This
is a particularly nice design.

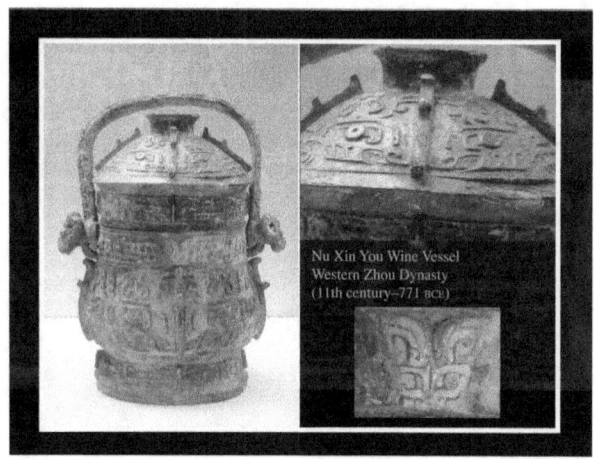

Nu Xin You Wine Vessel
Western Zhou Dynasty
(11th century–771 BCE)

我們在歷史的長河中不斷前行，現在我們從殷商王朝來到周朝。這是另外一件西周（西元前11世紀---西元前771年）出產的酒器。我們又看到每個酒器的頂上都佈滿了多種多樣的圖紋。頂上的這個的側面特別突出。

So, we move now from the Shang dynasty to the Zhou dynasty. We're moving forward in history. This is another wine vessel from the western Zhou, 11th century to 771 BCE. Again, we see multiple images stacked on top of each other. And this one on the top has a particularly striking profile.

側邊把手那裡，我們看到一種新的圖紋。這種圖紋，我們也將進一步探討。把手的側邊是一幅公羊紋，現在我們來探討把手上新的動物圖紋。

On the side, where the handles are, we see a new motif, which we'll also explore more. This is a ram on the side of the handle. So, now we'll explore this new motif of animals on the handles.

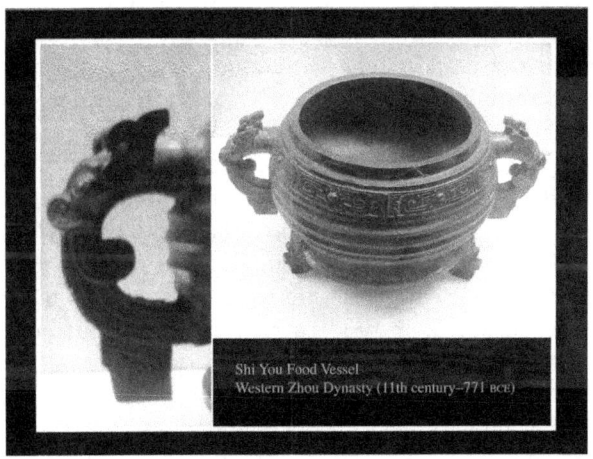

Shi You Food Vessel
Western Zhou Dynasty (11th century–771 BCE)

這裡我們有件西周（西元前11世紀---西元前771年）盛食物用的器皿--飯土硎。這裡的饕餮更像幾何圖形，更抽象了，很難認出它就是饕餮。這兒是側面，我們開始看到一些非常有趣的東西。而且我們還將看更多與此相關的圖紋。我們甚至看到一些像一頭馴鹿的圖紋，而且某種液體正從它的口中湧出來。可能這液體代表著水。這頭動物可能當作源泉；這液體也可能代表著血，這頭動物可能給人殺了。這是一頭鹿，是可食用動物。因此，這頭動物有可能被殺了當食物，或當宗教祭品。然而在古代文化裡，血象征著生命能量。因此，人們不會覺得這血跟現代恐怖片裡的血一樣可怕，而是被理解為生命能量的象徵，是生命能量的延續。舉例說，我記得道士劉明提及，據說周朝人們進行供奉和占卜的時候，為了能跟他們死去的祖先通靈，會將動物的喉嚨撕裂，讓動物因流血過多而死亡的同時，向喉嚨低語。即使到了今天，中國仙香的顏色還是黃色的，而香棍子是紅色的。這象徵著一隻喉嚨被割斷、雙腳被吊起來的雞。紅色的香棍子看起來像血。

Here we have a food vessel from the Western Zhou dynasty, 11th century to 771 BCE. Here the taotie is more geometric. It's more abstract. It's harder to identify it as the taotie. Here on the side, we begin to see something that's very interesting. And we'll see a lot more images that are very suggestive of this. We have what looks like it might even be a reindeer. And there is liquid pouring from its mouth. So, maybe this is meant to represent water. Maybe the animal is serving as a fountain. Maybe the liquid is meant to be blood. Maybe the animal is killed. This is a deer, which is a food animal. So, maybe the animal is killed for food or ritual purposes. Now, in ancient cultures, blood symbolized life force energy. So, blood wouldn't be considered scary, like it is in modern horror movies, but rather would be understood as a symbol for life energy. It's a symbol for the continuity of life energy. For example, I remember hearing a Taoist priest, Liu Ming, saying that in the Zhou dynasty sacrifices and oracle work, the priest would slit an animal's throat and whisper into the throat in order to communicate with their dead ancestors, as the animal was bleeding to death. Even today, Chinese incense sticks are yellow with a red stick. This is meant to symbolize a chicken with its throat cut which is strung up by its feet. The red stick is to resemble blood.

我們看這只像鹿的動物，它的鼻子上有一種非常有趣的渦紋裝飾。
我們會在本次演講裡看到更多鼻子上有渦紋裝飾的動物圖紋。

We can see that the nose of this deer-like animal has a very interesting spiral
motif. And we will see many more images that have this spiral motif on
their noses further on in the lecture.

此刻，我們正在構建一部視覺詞典。因此聽完本次演講後，你可以
去參觀一些博物館，例如殷墟博物院或河南省鄭州博物院，你可以
看著這些藝術作品，識別出它們的象徵意義。

Right now, we're building a visual vocabulary, so by the end of this lecture,
you'll be able to go to a museum, perhaps the museum at Yinxu or perhaps
the museum at Zhengzhou, Hunan Provincial Museum, and you'll be able
to look at the art and identify all of the symbolism. Also, you'll be able to
look at a lot of architecture in China and you'll see these recurring motifs.

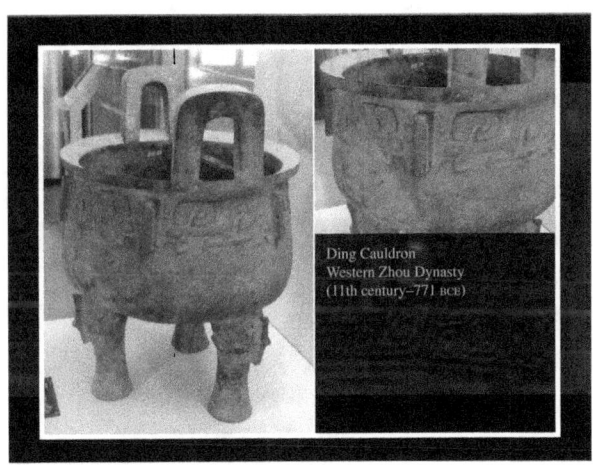

Ding Cauldron
Western Zhou Dynasty
(11th century–771 BCE)

西周時期（西元前11世紀到西元前771年）出現了鼎鑊。我們剛才
已經看過這類側面圖了。現在我們來看看饕餮紋的全圖。

From the western Zhou dynasty, 11th century to 771 BCE, we have a ding
cauldron. We've seen the side view before, and now this is the full image of
the taotie.

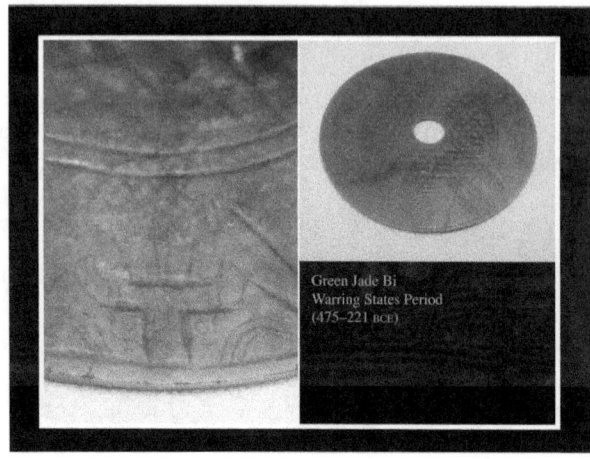

在歷史長河中繼續追溯，現在我們走進了戰國時代。這是一塊西元前475年到西元前221年的翡翠玉璧。在這塊玉體上，我們看到一幅圖紋，這讓我們再次想起了饕餮紋。

Moving forward in history, now we're in the Warring States period. This is a green jade bi from 475 to 221 BCE. On this jade object we have an image that, again, is suggestive of the taotie image.

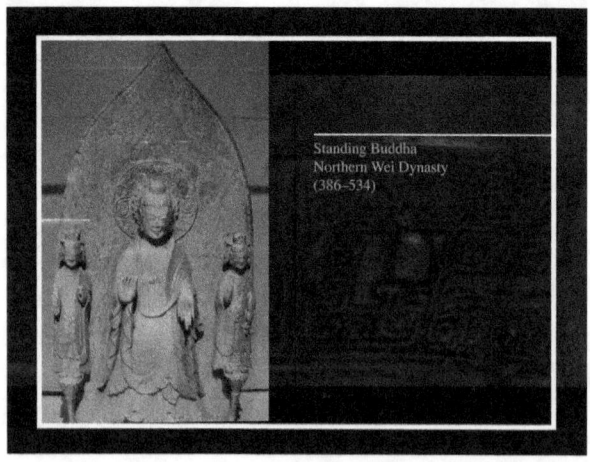

我們繼續追溯歷史，現在我們走進北魏（西元386年到西元534年）。這是一幅立式佛像圖。那麼，這佛像跟饕餮又有什麼關係呢？

Moving forward in history further, we are now in the northern Wei dynasty, 386 to 534. This is an image of a standing Buddha. Now what does the Buddha have to do with the taotie?

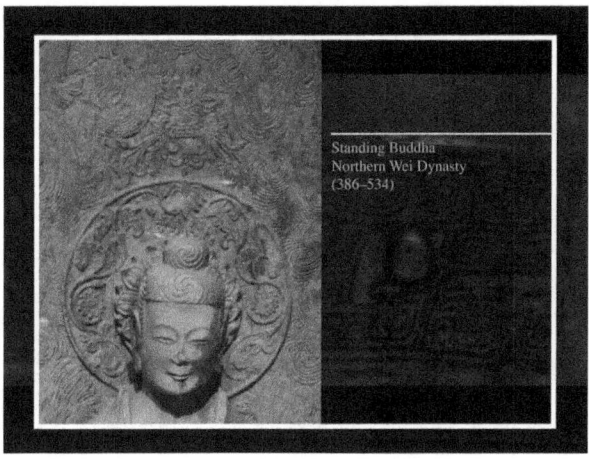

Standing Buddha
Northern Wei Dynasty
(386–534)

如果我們湊近圖看，我們會發現佛像的頭部的圖紋非常有趣。
When we look closely at the image we see a very interesting motif above the Buddha's head.

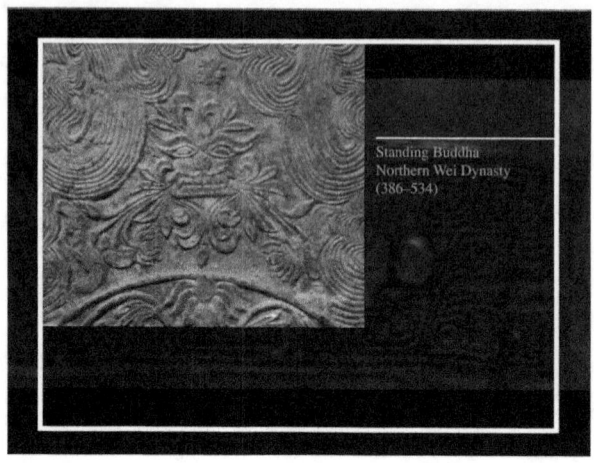

如果我們將圖像放大，我們會發現這圖紋跟饕餮非常像。不過存在不同之處。這幅圖是有下頜的，而且我們還看到一些新的圖紋。接下來我們會看到許多這種圖紋。我們看這花卉，這是花卉紋。這幅圖看上去跟饕餮很像的圖紋也許在吃花呢，或者也許在吐花。那些花要麼是被它吃進嘴裡，要麼是從它的嘴裡吐出來。它看起來簡直就像滴花。如果花是從它口中滴下來的話，這些花轉變成佛像的光暈，我們看見它也由同一種花卉紋組成的。

And when we enlarge the image we see that it is strikingly like the taotie. However, there are some differences. We see that this image has a bottom jaw. And we see some new motifs that we will see a lot more of in the future. We see flowers, a floral motif. This image that looks like the taotie is perhaps eating flowers. Or perhaps it is vomiting flowers. The flowers are either coming into its mouth or perhaps coming out of its mouth. It almost looks like its dripping flowers. And if its dripping flowers from its mouth, the flowers transform into the Buddha's halo which we see is made up of this same floral motif.

還有這幅圖，我喜歡看著佛像髮上的太極圖和頭飾。我認為藝術家加上這些圖紋相當巧妙，看上去很中國化。

Also, in this image, I enjoy seeing the taijitu symbol in the Buddha's hair and in the Buddha's top-knot. I think that's quite clever that the artist chose to add that. This is quite Chinese.

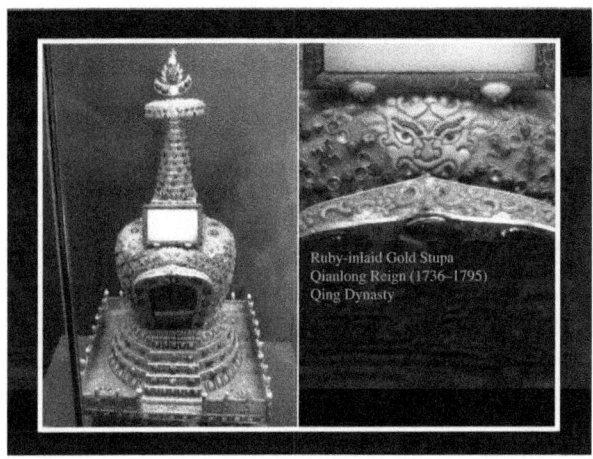

那麼，讓我們繼續追溯歷史。現在我們來到了清朝，清朝是中國歷上最後一個王朝。我們這裡有個鑲有紅寶石的金塔。這是一件佛教藝術品。我們看到這扇門口的上方的圖紋非常眼熟，它既像饕餮，也像那尊佛像上的圖紋。它也沒有下頜。另外，現在這幅圖與其說像一張動物臉，倒不如說更像一張惡魔臉。上面依然有花卉紋，花仿佛正從它嘴裡湧出來。花兒像水一樣從它的嘴裡湧出來。而且這幅圖也位於一扇門的上方，這圖紋更貼近於我們正在講敘的主題。我們再次構建一部視覺詞典。

So, let's move forward. We're already in the Qing dynasty, the last dynasty in China's dynastic period. Here we have a ruby-inlaid gold stupa. This is a piece of Buddhist art. What we see here above the doorway is this familiar-looking face. It is similar to both the taotie and the image we saw in the Buddhist sculpture. Again, there is no lower jaw. Also, the image now more resembles a demon face than an animal face. We still see the floral motif, the flowers that appear to be projecting from its mouth. Like water, flowers are pouring from its mouth. And this image is also above a doorway, which will become more relevant as we proceed. Again, we're building a visual vocabulary.

PART 2:
THE TAOTIE IMAGE IN THE CONTEXT OF SHANG COSMOLOGY AND PSYCHOLOGY

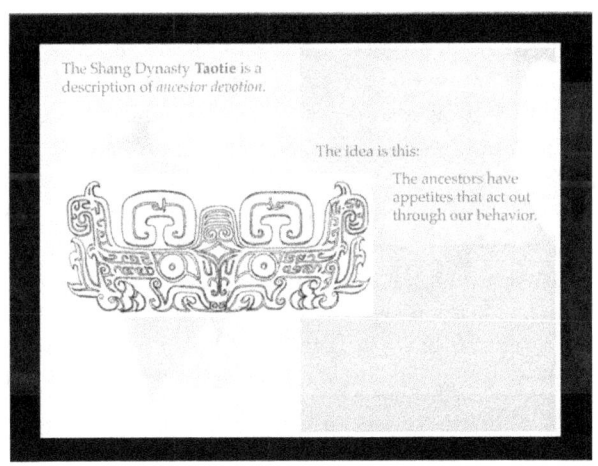

The Shang Dynasty **Taotie** is a description of *ancestor devotion*.

The idea is this:

The ancestors have appetites that act out through our behavior.

那麼，饕餮對殷商人來說有什麼象徵意義呢？ 如果我們生活在殷商時代，這種圖紋對我們來說意味著什麼呢？它跟我們的生活又有什麼關聯呢？

Now, what does the taotie image mean for Shang dynasty people? If we lived in the Shang dynasty, what would this image mean to us? What type of relevance would it have in our lives?

25

殷商時期，人們用饕餮是表達對祖先的崇拜之情。人們經常說"祖先敬奉"。不過我本人更喜歡用"祖先崇拜"這個詞。我覺得這個詞更貼切一些。我的想法是這樣的：祖先的欲望會在我們的行為中表現出來。比如，我的父親可能想要成為一名木匠，對嗎？因此每晚吃飯的時候，我的父親都會說他有多喜歡木工工程的事。因此，每晚吃飯的時候，我都得聽他說這些，對嗎？那麼，假如我的父親去世了，我長大之後開始想，也許我喜歡做些木工工程。由此可見，我父親、我祖父、我曾祖父的欲望影響了我的生活。這就是家庭的延續性。我們身上當然有基因的連續性，而且還擁有共同的觀念、家庭經歷、家庭文化、家庭利益和家庭價值觀。那麼，從過去到現在，在某種程度上，現代人提及祖先敬奉的時候，態度都是不屑的，有點看不起人。"清明節，燒紙錢祭祖,哈哈。"但是對祖先崇拜確實是件非常有意義的事。它表面的儀式之下有著複雜、美好而講究的東西。

The Shang dynasty taotie is a description of ancestral devotion. People often talk of ancestor worship. I prefer the term ancestor devotion. I feel that it's a little more accurate. The idea is this: the ancestors have appetites that act out through our behavior. So, perhaps my father wants to be a carpenter, right? So, every night at dinner my father always talks about how he would love to do carpentry work. So, every night at dinner I have to hear this, right? So, let's say my father passes away. And I grow up and I start thinking maybe I would like to do some carpentry work. So, the desires of my father, my grandfather, my great grandfather, they're relevant to my life. This is a family continuity. There's certainly a genetic continuity that we share. And there's also shared ideas, family stories, family culture, family beliefs, and family values. So, this moves from the past into the present. In a way, when modern people talk about ancestor worship they talk about it in a dismissive fashion and belittle people. "Qingming Festival. Burning things for ancestors, ha ha." But there really is a lot of sense to ancestor devotion. There is a complexity, beauty, and elegance to it beyond the surface of the rituals.

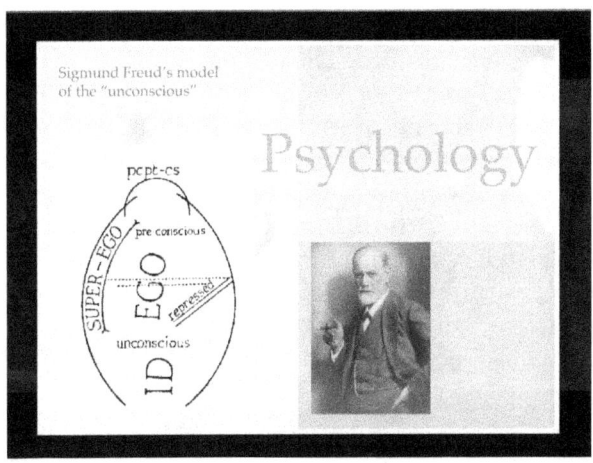

那麼，我們來談談饕餮在社群中起到的作用。它起到一種文化圖騰的作用，它幫助建立共同的文化認同感，在許多方面，它也是一種心理職能。在上面的那個例子中，比如我希望成為一名木匠，今天我可能認為那種欲望來自於我個人的潛意識。因此殷商人們的潛意識思維跟其先祖有關；因此先祖的想法跟潛意識思維非常接近。因為我們談到心理學，所以我們也許該來談談被譽為近代心理學之父的西格蒙德・佛洛德。佛洛德認為人的思維/靈魂就像一個雞蛋，或者好比一個裝滿了水的罐子。頂上的水很清澈，而底下的水很污濁，沉積著很多泥塵。每個人都有自我。自我是指"我"。這好比我們說，"我想吃餃子"。我們說"我"時，就是說自己想吃餃子。如果生活中有某些東西，比如性格特徵，令我們不舒服、被我們所否定，是我們傾向於拒絕的那部分自我。那些被我們拒絕的部分就成為潛意識。佛洛德認為許許多多潛意識的來源都跟我們的家庭有關，與我們家庭的動態、我們跟父母的關係有關。這是佛洛德的觀點。

So, in talking about the function that the taotie served in the community, it served as a cultural totem and helped create a shared sense of cultural identity, and in many ways it also served a psychological function. In the earlier example, my desire to become a carpenter, that is a desire that today I might think of as coming from the unconscious. So, the idea of the unconscious for the Shang relates to ancestors. So, the notion of what the ancestors are is very close to the idea of what the unconscious is. So, because we're talking about psychology, it's probably appropriate to talk a little about Sigmund Freud, who people call the father of modern psychology. Freud says that the mind, the psyche, is like an egg, or like a jar that is filled with water. And at the top, the water is very clear. While at the bottom, the water is very murky and dark. There's a lot of mud in the water at the bottom. We have the ego. The ego means "I". It's what we identify with when we say, "I like to eat jiaozi." We're saying "I", the ego, likes to eat jiaozi. If there is something in our life that we have, a character trait perhaps, that we're not comfortable with, that isn't what we identify with. That's what we dis-identify with. That's those parts of ourselves that we tend to reject. And those parts that we reject become the unconscious. And a lot of this unconscious material, Freud says, relates to our family. It relates to our family dynamic: our relationship with our mother and our relationship with our father. This is what Freud says.

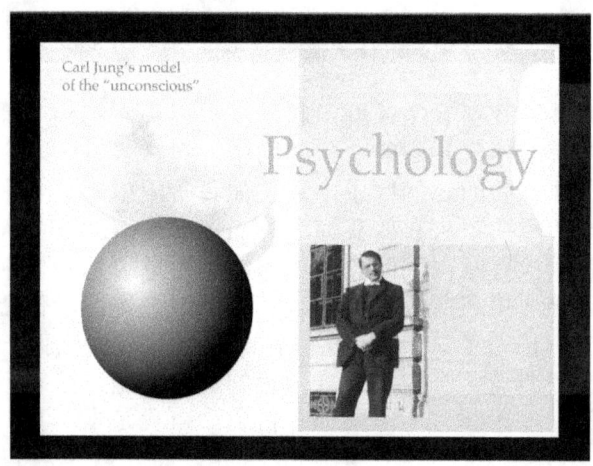

繼佛洛德之後，我們這裡有卡爾·榮格，有卡爾·榮格關於思維和潛意識的原型。卡爾·榮格認為思維/精神就像一個球體。球體表面光的反射就像自我，也存在潛意識，它是所有灰色區域。球體那些暗區就代表著潛意識，是指思維中那些無意識的部分。

Here we have Carl Jung. Carl Jung came after Freud. Here's Carl Jung's model of the psyche and the unconscious. Carl Jung says that the psyche, the mind, is like a sphere. And the reflection of light on the surface of the sphere is like the ego. There is also the subconscious, which is all the grey area, while the area on the sphere that is dark represents the unconscious, those parts of the psyche that we're not consciously aware of.

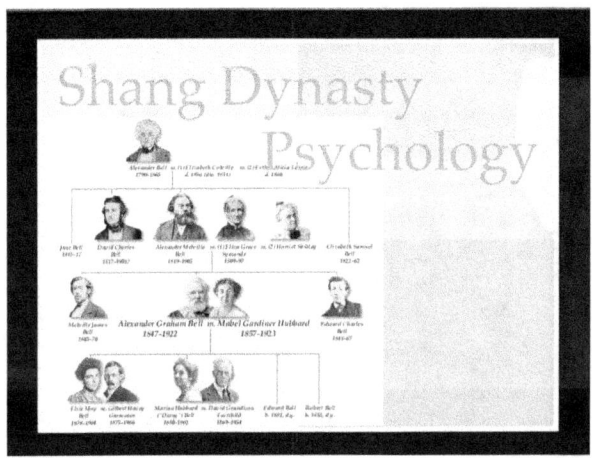

繼佛洛德之後，我們這裡有卡爾・榮格，有卡爾・榮格關於思維和潛意識的原型。卡爾・榮格認為思維／精神就像一個球體。球體表面光的反射就像自我，也存在潛意識，它是所有灰色區域。球體那些暗區就代表著潛意識，是指思維中那些無意識的部分。

So here we are. Let's do our best to imagine Shang dynasty psychology. Here's a person, here's his parents, his grandparents, his great grandparents. We have a family system here. For the Shang, this family system, the ancestors, represents the unconscious because the desires of the ancestors are the unconscious.

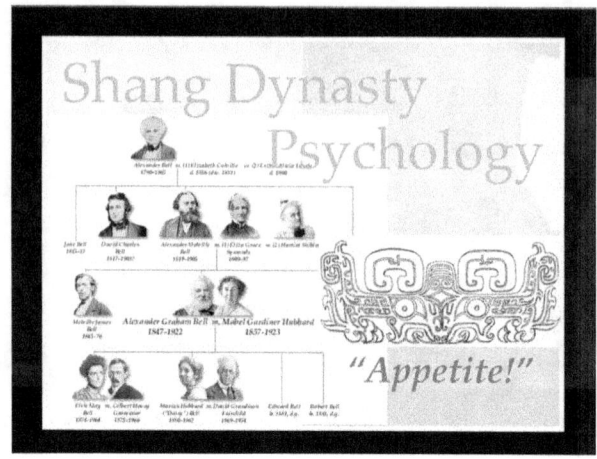

祖先的表現是以欲望的形式表現出來的。比如說，假設喬叔叔有了外遇。所有人都搖頭，表示不認同他這種行為。他們說，"喬叔叔，你怎能做這種事？" 喬叔叔說，"我不知道驅使我這樣做的力量來自哪裡。" 殷商人會說，"嗯，力量來自于你的祖先，因為你的父親、祖父或者曾祖父死後未得償所願。他們仍有欲望，他們的欲望就通過你表現出來了。" 所以，殷商人是這樣理解潛意識和人類行為的，特別是對那些難以理解的人類行為，他們就理解為祖先的欲望。

The ancestors express, and they express as appetite. So, for example, perhaps Uncle Joe is having an affair. Everyone shakes their head. They says, "Uncle Joe how could you do such a thing?" Uncle Joe says, "I don't know where this energy is coming from." The Shang would say, "Well, this energy comes from the ancestors, because your father, grandfather, or great grandfather was not resolved after death. They still have appetite and their appetite is expressing through you." So, that's how the Shang dynasty people understood the unconscious, how they understood human behavior, particularly those parts of human behavior that are difficult to understand. It's the appetite of ancestors.

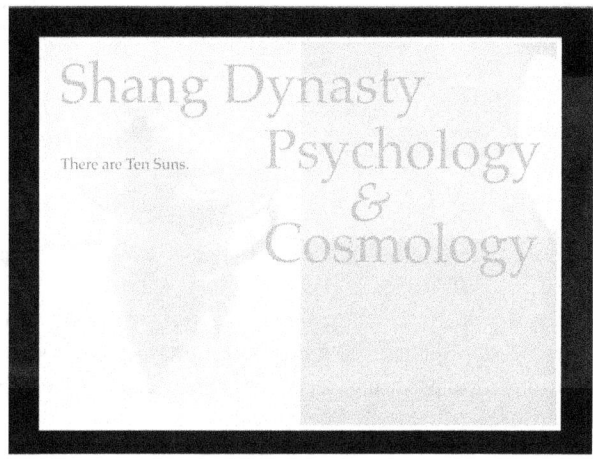

這裡我們有與宇宙論有關的殷商心理學，在遠古時代，全世界的心理學和宇宙論實際上都是一樣的。對我們來說，這是一種很難理解的思維。可是在遠古世紀的人們就是這樣認為的。比如說，殷商人認為天上有十個太陽。

Here we have the Shang dynasty psychology as it relates to cosmology. Now in the ancient world, all over the world, really, psychology and cosmology were the same. For us, this is a very difficult idea to understand. But this is the way that people thought in the ancient world. So, for the Shang there are ten suns.

我們可能會想起神話故事《後羿射日》中所說的那十個太陽，因為天上有十個太陽，後羿才將其中九個射下來了。那麼，這為什麼呢？我想這是因為《後羿射日》這個神話與周朝人們戰勝商朝有關。這是我的看法。

And we might think of the ten suns in the Houyi myth, because there are ten suns and Houyi shoots down nine. Now why is that? I think it's because the Houyi myth relates to the Zhou people conquering the Shang. That's my belief.

殷商人之所以認為天上有十個太陽，是因為殷商時期的曆法是陽
曆。還有他們的陽曆裡，一周有十天。現在我們是七天為一周。因
為殷商時期一周有十天，所以他們一周的時間比我們長。對於他們
來說，一周裡的每天都是為某位特定的祖先而設定的。所以也許星
期一代表祖父，也許星期二代表祖母，也許星期三代表曾祖父等
等。

So, for the Shang there are ten suns, because the Shang have a solar
calendar. And in their solar calendar they have a ten-day week. Now, we
have a seven-day week. Since the Shang had ten, they had a longer week
than us. For them, each day of the week is designated to a specific ancestral
relationship. So maybe Monday represents grandfather. Maybe Tuesday
represents grandmother. Maybe Wednesday represents great grandfather.
And so on.

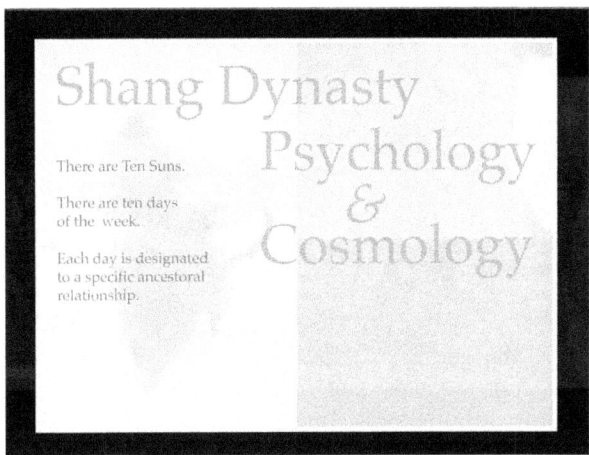

宇宙論認為太陽跟一周的日子有關，還跟祖先的關係有關。舉例說，人們會虔誠地祭祀祖先。今天我們看到人們在佛寺和道觀揮香，對嗎？殷商期間，人們一周裡的每天都會為一位元特定的祖先舉行一種類似的儀式。他們舉行這種儀式的時候，心裡會想，想念著這位特定的祖先。因此，這些宗教儀式其實是一種心理活動。這些儀式是跟這些祖先建立聯繫的一種途徑，是人們跟其祖先不同的性格特徵建立聯繫的一種途徑。因此，我們看看它是如何擔當心理職能的。它一點都不顯淺，這裡有某些相當深奧東西。

The suns relate to the days of the week, which is cosmology, and they also relate to ancestral relationships. For example, what people would do is they would do devotional sacrifices. Today you see people waving incense at the Buddhist or Taoist temple, right? During Shang times, people would have a similar ritual every day of the week for a specific ancestral relationship. And when they would do these activities they would think, they would meditate, on that specific ancestral relationship. So, these rituals, really, were a type of psychology. These rituals were a way of building a relationship with these different ancestors. It's a way that people were building a relationship with different aspects of their own personality. So, we can see how it did serve a psychological function. It's not superficial. There's something here that's quite profound.

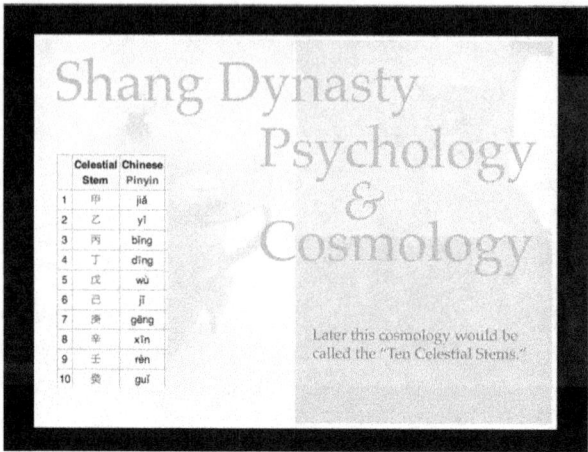

後來，繼商朝之後，殷商宇宙論在漢朝時用漢字表達為＂十天干＂，它成了道教占星術中的一部分。我們這裡有＂十天干＂的漢字寫法，也有＂十天干＂的拼音寫法。＂十天干＂的概念甚至沿用至今。商朝的曆法是陽曆，周朝的曆法是陰曆。此後的各朝代都混合了陰曆和陽曆。比如說，清明節是一個陽曆節氣，陰曆和陽曆是貫穿在一起的。

Later, after the Shang dynasty, in the Han dynasty, the cosmology of the Shang is called the ten celestial stems, and is incorporated into Taoist astrology. Here we have the ten celestial stems in Chinese characters and here we have them in pinyin. Even this notion of ten has a continuity to the present. The Shang had a solar calendar. The Zhou had a lunar calendar. And every dynasty since has had a lunar-solar calendar. Qingming Festival, for example, is a solar holiday. The two calendars intersect.

PART 3:
THE TAOTIE IMAGE FROM A CROSS CULTURAL PERSPECTIVE:
— SECTION 1: INDIA —

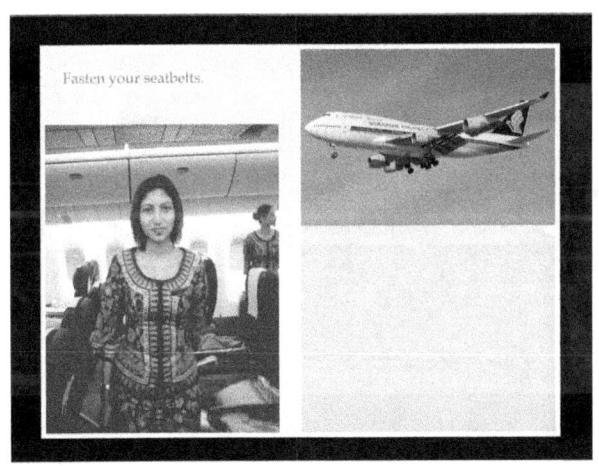

既然比較法對象徵意義的研究非常重要。那麼現在請將託盤桌子折疊好，椅背調到直立位置，系好你的座位安全帶，祝你旅途愉快。因為我們即將飛往印度。關於饕餮圖紋，印度能帶給我們一種跨文化的透視。

Now, there is a great deal of value to a comparative approach to symbolic studies, so secure your tray tables, put your seats in an upright position, fasten your seatbelts and tighten it, and have a pleasant journey, because we are going to fly to India. And India will give us a cross-cultural perspective on the taotie image.

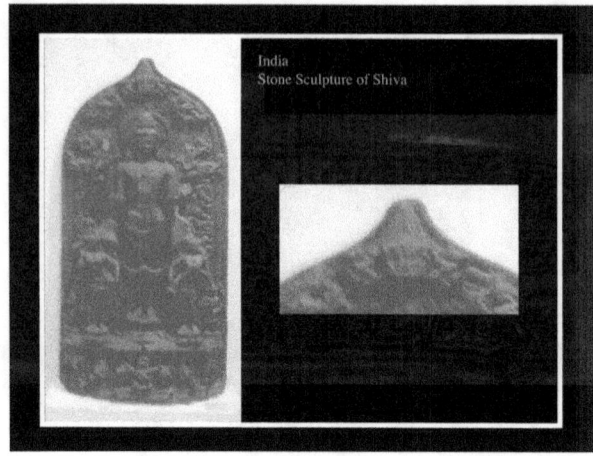

這裡我們看到一尊濕婆神石雕。我們看見天神的頭上有一幅圖紋，很抱歉，照片的品質比較差，不過天神的頭上有幅圖紋，看上去有點像饕餮。濕婆神頭頂上的光暈是錐形的，仿佛是從上方的圖紋中滴下來那樣，我們還記得之前那尊中國佛像上的光暈，看上去也像是從上方的圖紋中滴下來那樣。

Here we see a stone sculpture of the god Shiva. Above the god's head we see an image, and I apologize for the poor quality of the photograph, but above the god's head is an image that looks a little like the taotie. And the halo of the god Shiva is tapered at the top. It is almost as if the halo is dripping from the image above it. And we remember how, earlier, in the Chinese Buddhist statue the halo looked like it was dripping from the image above it.

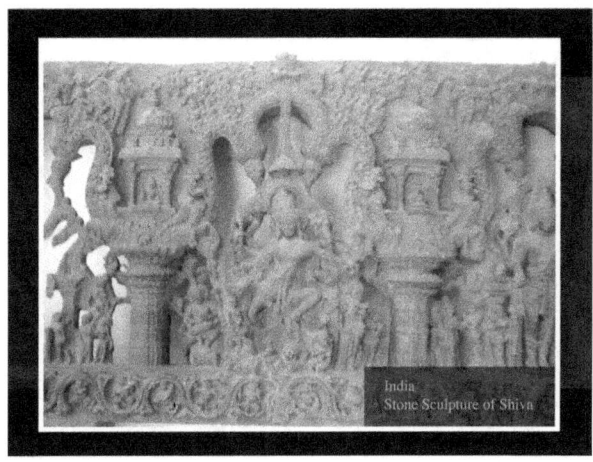

這裡有張清晰點的照片，圖紋非常接近，或者其實是一樣的。我們再看看濕婆神，它上方的圖紋跟饕餮是很相似的：有驚人雙眼、那是一雙掠奪者的大眼，沒有下頜，長著獠牙。不同的是，濕婆神上方滴下來的是一把遮陽傘，一把雨傘，而不是光暈。遮陽傘跟光暈的作用是一樣的，很顯然是用來滴向它的。你可以看見它是如何像布塊或能量：火或水那樣向下延伸。它跟那尊佛像上方的那幅圖紋一樣從這裡向左右兩邊延伸。還有花卉紋，有趣的是，花卉紋是如何向下滴在左右兩邊的怪獸圖紋上的呢。

This is a better photograph of a similar, or really the same, motif. Again, we have the god Shiva. Again, we have the image above it that resembles the taotie. It has these striking eyes, large predator eyes. It has no lower jaw. It has fangs. Instead of the halo it is dripping a parasol, an umbrella, above the deity Shiva. The parasol serves the same function as a halo. It's visibly dripping it. You can see how it extends down like pieces of cloth or energy, fire, or water. Here, extending out to the left and right, like in the image above the Chinese Buddha, there is a floral motif. And an interesting thing is how the floral motif drips down toward these monster images on the left and right.

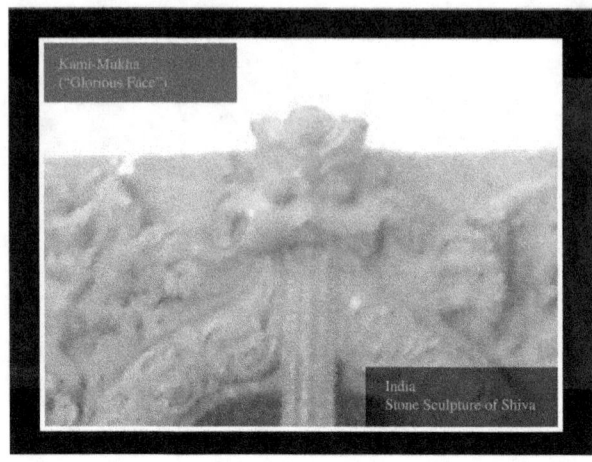

那麼，這傢伙是誰呀？形態類似饕餮，可是它在印度中又有何象徵意義呢？在印度，這種圖紋叫加美穆哈，它是"榮耀之臉"的意思。還有在印度《愛經》裡"Kami"這個詞跟"kama"有關，這詞是"欲望"的意思。因此，加美穆哈暗示著"欲望之臉"。"欲望"也被理解為"饑餓"。然而，中國的饕餮代表的欲望----祖先的欲望，而在印度，加美穆哈也代表著欲望----生物學上的欲望，代表著生存欲望的滿足。

So, who is this guy? This image resembles the taotie, but what does it mean in India? In India, this image is called the kami-mukha, the "face of glory". Also, the word kami relates to the word kama, as in Kamasutra, which means desire. So, the name kami mukha is suggestive of "face of desire". Desire is also understood as hunger. So, whereas, the taotie in China represents appetite, the appetites of ancestors, in India, the kami-mukha also represents appetite, the appetites of biology. It represents the insatiable appetite of life.

這裡有個關於加美穆哈的故事，還有他跟濕婆神的關係。因此，我現在就給你們講述這個故事。有一天，所有小神聚一起玩耍嬉戲，突然來了個巨人，這個巨人開始侵擾他們的生活，開始毆打他們，他們越來越害怕，這位巨人讓他們的生活苦不堪言。於是他們去濕婆神那裡去尋求幫助。他們說，"我們那裡有個怪獸，是個巨人，他老是毆打我們。請幫幫我們吧。"於是濕婆神說，"好吧，我來幫你們！"說完他馬上運用第三隻眼創造了另一頭怪獸。因此，現在就有了兩隻怪獸。濕婆神對第二頭怪獸說，"你的職責就是將第一頭怪獸吃掉。"所以，第二頭怪獸的樣子異常恐怖。他在第一頭怪獸的後面窮追不捨。第一頭怪獸感到越來越害怕。於是他跑到濕婆神面前說，"請幫幫我。那頭怪獸要吃我！"於是濕婆神說，"好吧，你現在安全了。只要你做個好巨人，另外一頭怪獸是不會傷害你的。"不過，現在我們出現了一個問題，因為濕婆神之前告訴第二頭怪獸說它的職責就是將第一頭怪獸吃掉。因此第二頭怪獸會怎麼做呢？第二頭怪獸說，"我生來就是為了吃而存在。我的生活除了無情的饑餓之外，一無所有。除了饑餓，我別的什麼都不知道。我應該怎麼辦呀？"於是濕婆神說，"吃你自己吧。"於是那頭怪獸抓住自己的腳，將它塞進了自己的嘴裡，開始吃了起來，接著它又抓住自己的腿，將腿塞進了自己的嘴裡，又開始吃了起來。接著是臀部、胸部、手臂等等所有部位，最後甚至連下頜都吃光了，只剩下它自己的頭。濕婆神目睹這一切後說，"唔，這樣子看起來其實很美很有深意。以後你就叫做加美穆哈吧，是光榮之臉的意思，因為你反映了真實生活的境象！因為處於生物級別的生命就是為了饑餓而存在。"所有生物生命都因食欲和饑餓而存在。我們擁有身體是因為我們渴望食物，渴望水。為了生存，我們必須有想睡覺的欲望。實際上睡覺也是一種欲望。試著不去睡覺，好比試著不去吃東西一樣，是完全行不通的。我曾聽聞，我們所有人的父母都有性欲，要不是這樣的話，我們就不會出現在這裡。因此生物生命的基本因素是饑餓、欲望。在印度藝術和印度肖像研究中，那就是這圖像所要表達的象徵意義。而且它還跟饕餮很相似，對嗎？

There is a story about the kami-mukha and its relationship to the god Shiva. So, I'll tell you that story right now. There were all of these minor deities, they're having a nice day. And all of a sudden there is a titan that begins to harass them and begins to beat them up. And they become so terrified by this titan that's making their lives miserable that they go to this god, the god Shiva, for help. And they say, "There's a monster, a titan, that's beating us up. Help us." So, the god Shiva says, "Okay. I'll help you." And, out of his third eye he creates another monster. So, now there's two monsters. The god Shiva tells this second monster, "It's your function to eat the first monster." So, the second monster is very scary looking. He runs at the first monster. The first monster get's frightened. He runs to the god Shiva and says, "Please help me. This monster is going to eat me." So, the god Shiva says, "Okay. You're safe. Be a good titan and this other monster won't hurt you." But now, we have a problem, because he told the second monster that it's his job to eat the first one. So, what's the second monster going to do? The second monster says, "I exist to eat. My life is nothing but unrelenting hunger. Hunger is all I know. What am I going to do?" So the god Shiva says, "Eat yourself." So, the monster grabs its feet, puts its feet into its mouth and starts eating. It grabs its legs, puts its legs into its mouth and begins eating. It's butt, its chest, its arms, everything, even the lower jaw. The top of its head is all that's left. Now, the god Shiva sees this and says, "Hmm, this is actually quite beautiful and profound. I will call you kami-mukha, face of glory, because you represent an image of what life is! Because life, at the biological level, exists because of hunger. All biological life is appetite and hunger. We have bodies because we hunger for food. We hunger for water. To live, we have to have an appetite for sleep. Even sleep is an appetite. Try to go without sleep as you might try to go without food. It won't work. I have heard that all of our parents had an appetite for sex, otherwise we wouldn't be here. So the foundation of all biological life is hunger, appetite. So, that's what this image means in Indian art and Hindu iconography. And it's very similar to the taotie, right?

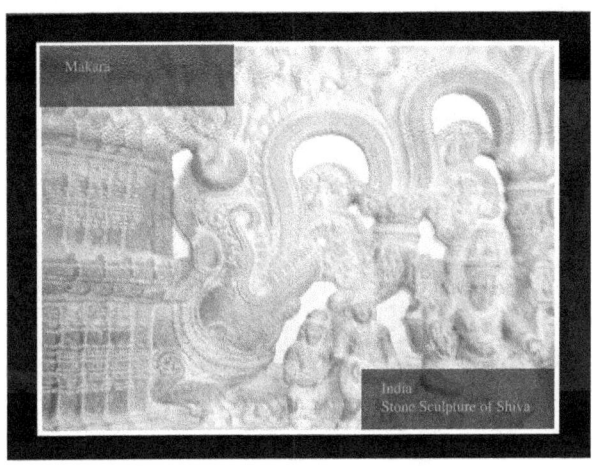

啊，那麼我們記住這幅圖紋。我們看看這花卉紋，它一路向下來延伸到這怪獸的頭。因此，這裡有個怪獸頭的特寫。它的名字叫摩伽羅。 摩伽羅是印度藝術的一個象徵。它是一頭神話中的怪獸，代表著饑餓，代表著欲望。我們似乎在談論一些類似的主題。在印度文化裡，這個象徵是這樣用的。假設有一個印第安小男孩，這個小男孩說，"媽咪，媽咪，媽咪，給我更多食物，給我更多食物。"於是那位媽媽說，"啊，你就像個摩伽羅。"永無止境的欲望，因此摩伽羅再次被當著勸誡的象徵來用。我們用它說，"不，別像個摩伽羅，別太貪婪，別總是渴求某樣東西。"因為如果我們總是渴求某樣東西的話，會讓我們喪失人性，對嗎？那有點瘋狂。

Ah, so we remember this image. We see that the floral motif goes down to here, this monster head. So, here is a close up of the monster head. This is called a makara. The makara is a symbol in Indian art. It's a mythological monster and it represents hunger. It represents appetite. It seems we are talking about some similar themes. In Indian culture the symbol is used like this. Imagine a little Indian boy. And the boy says, "Mommy, mommy, mommy, give me more food. Give me more food." And the mother says, "Ah. You act just like a makara." Unending appetite. So again, the makara is used as a cautionary symbol. We use it to say, "No. Don't act like a makara. Don't be greedy. Don't be always hungry for something." Because we loose our humanity if we're always hungry for something. Right? That's a little crazy.

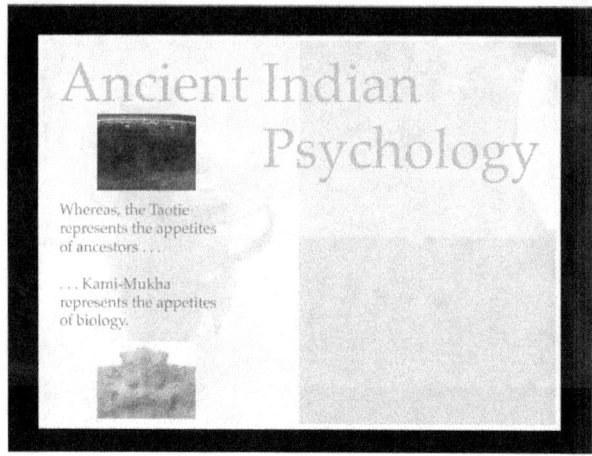

關於古印度心理學，我們說過佛洛伊德心理學，我們說過榮格心理
學，我們說過殷商心理學，天啊，現在是古印度心理學。因此饕餮
代表祖先的欲望，加美穆哈代表生物的欲望：食物，水，睡眠和性。
Ancient Indian psychology. We talked about Freudian psychology. We
talked about Jungian psychology. We talked about Shang dynasty
psychology. Goodness gracious, now we have ancient Indian psychology.
Whereas the taotie represents the appetites of ancestors, the kami-mukha
represents the appetites of biology. Food, water, sleep, sex.

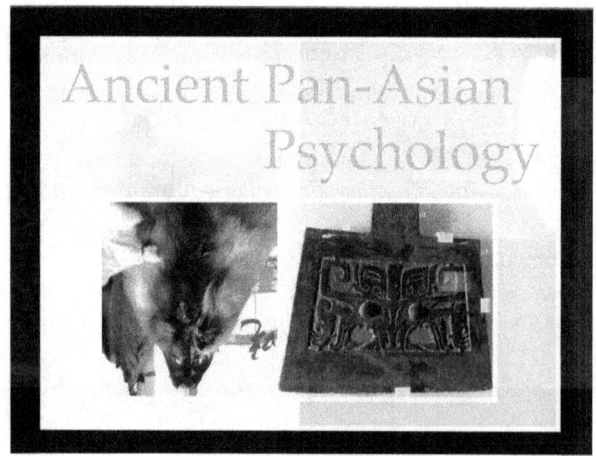

那麼，現在我們明白了古泛亞心理學的象徵意義，它可能萌牙於舊石器時代，因此可能很古老很古老了。

So, what we have is the suggestion of an ancient pan-Asian psychology. Which probably comes from the Paleolithic, so it's probably very very old.

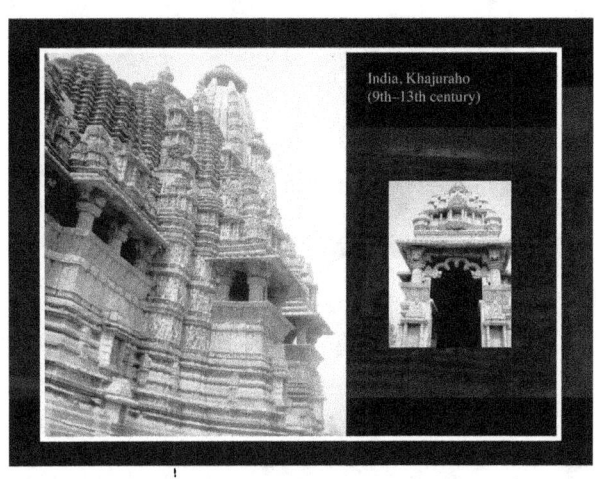

我們印度這裡有雄偉壯觀的神廟。印度卡朱拉霍那裡就有一座9世紀到13世紀的濕婆神廟，那是一群龐大的建築物。

So, here we have a huge temple in India. This is a Shiva temple in Khajuraho, India, 9th to 13th centuries. It's enormous.

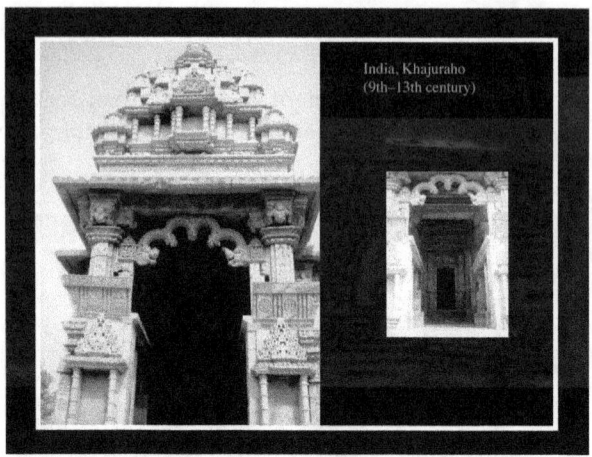

這裡是神廟的正面，我們拉近來看看，好嗎？是的，讓我們拉近一點。

Here, is the front of the temple. Shall we move closer? Yeah, let's move closer.

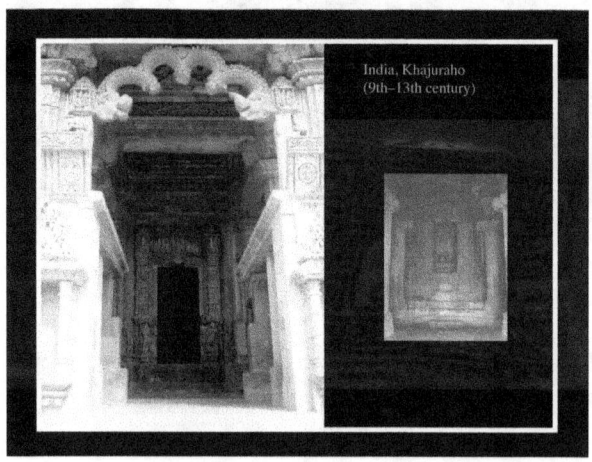

現在，這裡是正門入口，我們看到門口上方是加美穆哈，兩側是摩伽羅。加美穆哈向左右兩邊輸出能量，這些能量傾注在摩伽羅像上。這個摩伽羅長著象鼻般的鼻子。

Now, at the front entrance we see above the doorway the kami-mukha and the two makaras on the side. So, to the left and right, pouring out of the kami-mukha we have this outpouring of energy that goes to the makara images. The makaras here have an elephant-like nose.

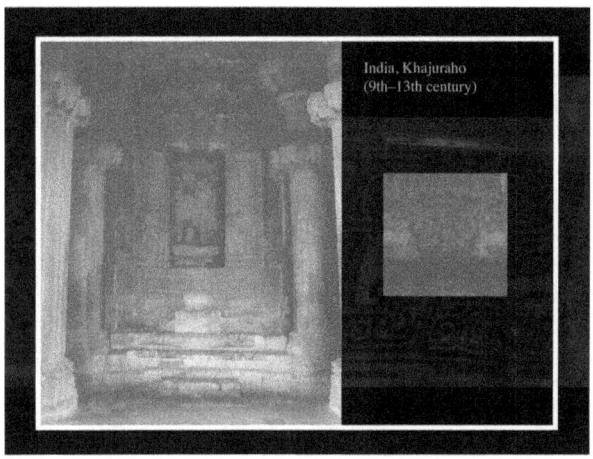

我們進去好嗎？你拿手電筒了嗎？因為要進去的話，我們要有手電筒才行。現在我們來到神廟的中心。這裡是神廟最深入內部的中心神殿。門口之上有幅加美穆哈像。如果你記得那座清朝佛塔的話，你會記得佛塔門口上方那種跟饕餮類似的圖紋的樣子。在印度藝術中，濕婆神廟的門口上總能看到加美穆哈像，它是濕婆神廟的組成部分。我們在中心神殿的門內外上方都看到加美穆哈像。那麼能出現在神廟中心的圖像，對印度人們來說一定非常重要。所以，我再次想知道不同文化的透視能否帶給我們更多的線索，讓我們弄明白這圖的象徵意義？

Shall we go inside? Did you bring your flashlights? Because we'll need flashlights to go inside. We are now in the heart of the temple. Here is the central shrine in the deepest interior part of the temple. Above the doorway we have the kami-mukha image. Now, if you remember the Buddhist stupa from the Qing dynasty, you'll remember how we saw the image that resembled the taotie above the doorway of the stupa. So, here in Indian art, above the doorways in Shiva temples we consistently see the kami-mukha image. It's part of a Shiva temple. We see it above the doorway out front and also above the doorway of the inner sanctum, the heart of the temple. So, if this image is in the heart of the temple, it must be very important to people in India. So, I wonder if, again, a cross-cultural perspective can give us some more clues to what this image means?

PART 4:
THE TAOTIE IMAGE FROM A CROSS CULTURAL PERSPECTIVE:
— SECTION 2: NEPAL —

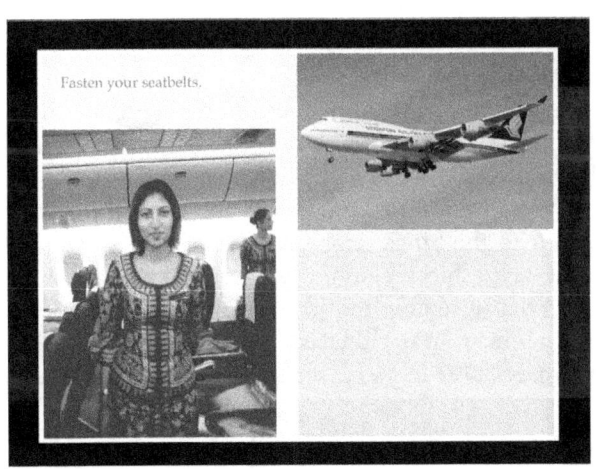

既然如此，請將託盤桌子折疊好，椅背調到直立位置，系好你們的座位安全帶，祝你們旅途愉快。因為我們即將飛往尼泊爾。

So, fasten your seatbelts, secure your tray tables, put your seats in an upright position, and enjoy your flight, because we are flying to Nepal.

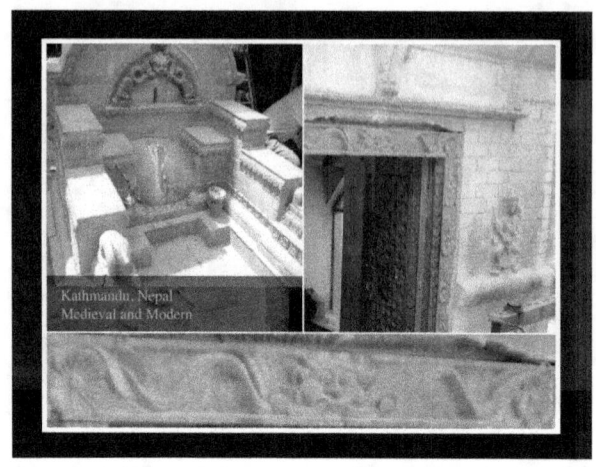

現在我們來到尼泊爾的加德滿都。這是一座象頭神的小神廟。誰看過那位長著象頭的印度神衹？它是格涅沙。這裡是一座用來供奉那位神衹的神廟。這兒，就在這裡，是一座小濕婆神廟。跟象頭神廟一樣，我們在濕婆神廟的門上方也看到了加美穆哈像。上面有蛇，有花，是一幅花卉圖紋，你們會記得在後來那些類似於饕餮的中國圖紋上，我們在那尊佛像上看到的花卉紋。那些圖像要麼是在吞花，要麼是在吐花。我們在尼泊爾這裡也看到同樣的東西，你們看到這些花了嗎？

So, here we are now in Kathmandu, Nepal. This is a small shrine to the god Ganesh. Who has seen the Indian deity with the elephant head? That's Ganesh. This is a shrine to that deity. This, right here, is a small Shiva temple. So, just as on the shrine to Ganesh we see the kami-muka image. So too, on the door to the Shiva temple we see it again. And we have snakes and flowers, a floral motif. And you'll remember in some of the late Chinese images that resemble the taotie, that we saw a floral motif above the Buddha. The image was either eating flowers or flowers were coming out of its mouth. So, here in Nepal we see the same thing. See the flowers?

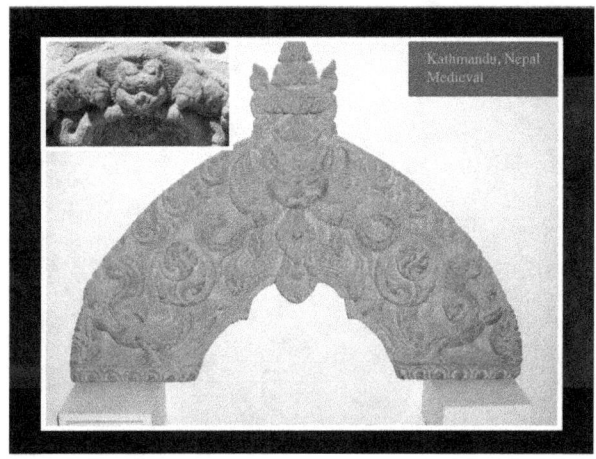

這裡又出現了加美穆哈像，嘴裡湧著蛇和花卉。這些蛇和花卉傾倒在這些摩伽羅的身上。尼泊爾的摩伽羅看上去非常漂亮，你們看摩伽羅的鼻子，你們看它的腳。我們又看到這種圖紋了。看看它的爪子和筆直豎向空中的尾巴。我們還在別的什麼地方看過長有小爪，尾巴筆直豎向空中，長著獠牙的臉呢？

Here is the kami-mukha again, with snakes and flowers pouring out of its mouth. And they pour down to these makaras. Nepal has some very beautiful makara images. Look at the makara's nose. Look at it's foot. We'll see this image again. Look at it's jaws and its tail going straight up in the air. Where else have we seen fanged faces with a little claw and a tail that goes straight up in the air?

下一幅圖是刻在石上的加美穆哈像。

This next image is a kami-mukha in stone.

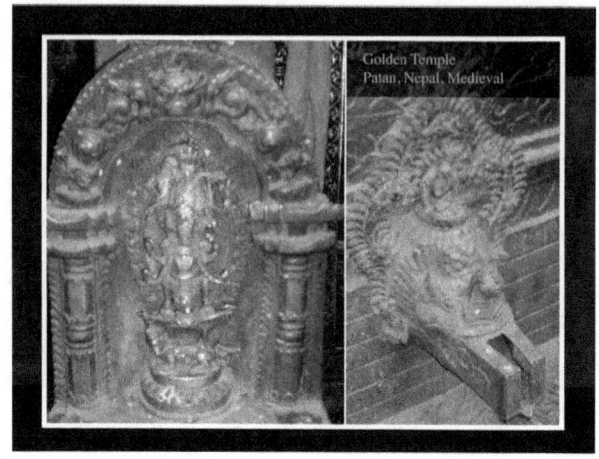

這些是尼泊爾帕坦裡的圖像。這裡是一座非常漂亮的佛寺，叫黃金寺。寺裡有座小神廟，圖像的上方，我們再次看到加美穆哈。你們看它的鼻子，是如此特別啊！這裡我們看到一個摩伽羅像。在尼泊爾，噴泉上面也有摩伽羅像。所有尼泊爾境內的古老噴泉都是摩伽羅像的造型。記好了，摩伽羅代表永無止境的欲望、饑餓、食欲。可是這圖像也被用來造噴泉。噴泉每天都有水湧噴而出。如果我們生活在中世紀的帕坦，我們每次去噴泉洗澡或挑飲用水時，都可以從這象徵物的口中取水。代表永無止境的欲望的象徵物餵養著我們，它讓我們想起了生命的生物級別。

So, these images are in Patan, Nepal. This is at a very nice Buddhist temple called the Golden Temple. And it has a small shrine here and above the image, again, we see the kami-mukha. Look at its snout, it's so distinctive. Here we see a makara. In Nepal we also have the makara image on fountains. All of the old fountains in Nepal are styled after the makara image. Now remember, that the makara represents unceasing desire, hunger, appetite. And yet this image is used as a fountain. It is pouring forth water every day. If we lived in Patan, in Medieval times, every time we went to the fountain to bathe, or to collect water to drink, we would get it from the mouth of a symbol. We would be fed from a symbol that represents unceasing desire. It reminds us of the biological level of being.

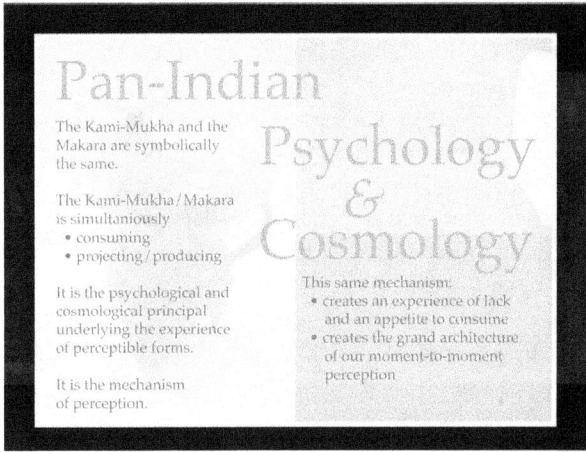

現在，讓我們思考一下泛神論和宇宙論。加美穆哈和摩伽羅的象徵意義是一樣的，因為它們兩都都代表著饑餓、食欲和欲望。這裡會更複雜一些。加美穆哈/摩伽羅既消耗又供給/生產。它既侵食，卻也是源泉，因為它將吃進去的東西倒出來。因此它既吸引能量，也輸出同一種能量。就像陰/陽，施/受那樣。這幅圖表現了生活的兩個方面。泛印度心理學中，加美穆哈和摩伽羅被理解為以可感知形式經驗為基礎的心理和宇宙論原則。這是一種感知機制。因此我是這樣想的，我可能感覺到饑餓，我可能在欲望，我可能還沒吃飯，於是我說，"我餓了，我肚子空空的，我要填飽它。"因此，我餓了這一概念是客體內容。可是這裡是思維。加美穆哈/摩伽羅隱藏在知覺經驗的思想內容之下。它在思想內容的下面。我們生活經驗的主體內容來源於某處，這就是它的來源。認識和感知是我們生活經驗的基礎。發生在我們身上的事是我們的意識使然，我們的知覺經驗是以我們生活中發生的事情為基礎。我們有思維，思維是事物，但是事物表面之下和思維表面之下隱藏著感知機制。

Now, let's consider pan-Indian psychology and cosmology. The kami-mukha and the makara are symbolically the same, because they both represent hunger, appetite, and desire. It's a little more complex here. The kami-mukha/makara is simultaneously consuming and projecting/producing. It is eating and yet it is also a fountain. It is pouring forth. So, the same energy that gives, also takes. It's like the yin/yang. There's a giving and a receiving. There are two aspects of life that are represented in this one image. In pan-Indian psychology the kami-mukha and makara is understood as the psychological and cosmological principle underlying the experience of perceptible forms. It is the mechanism of perception. So, the idea is this. I might have hunger. I might have appetite. I might not have had dinner and I say, "I am hungry. I am empty. I need to be filled." So, the notion of my hunger, that is content. But here's the idea, the kami-mukha/makara is underneath the idea of the content of our experience of perception. It's below it. The content of our experiences in life comes from somewhere and this is where it comes from. Awareness and perception underlie the experiences of our lives. Beneath the things that happen to us is our awareness. Our experience of consciousness is underneath the things that happen in our life. I have ideas. Ideas are things. But beneath things, beneath ideas, is the mechanism of perception.

對心理學的這種理解，真正重要的是，西格蒙德·佛洛德或卡爾·榮格會談論你生活的主體內容，"你跟父母是什麼關係？"（佛洛伊德心理學），這種心理學的古老解釋受思維水準、形式和主休內容等層面的限制，沒有戲劇，沒有情工節，其實這是仲介層面上的東西。

What's really significant here in this understanding of psychology is that, whereas Sigmund Freud or Carl Jung will talk about the content of your life, "What is your relationship with your parents?" (Freudian Psychology), this ancient understanding of psychology is below the level of ideas, form, and content. There is no drama there. There are no stories. Really, this is at the level of mediation.

同樣地---這種無縫意識---造成經驗不足和產生食欲，也產生我們隨時可見的宏偉建築。這種基本的意識經驗受生活的欲望限制，也受我們每時每刻的觀念所支配。

The same mechanism—this seamless awareness—which creates an experience of lack and an appetite to consume, also creates the grand architecture of our moment-to-moment perception. This base experience of awareness is below the appetites of life and it is also below the projection of our moment-to-moment perceptions.

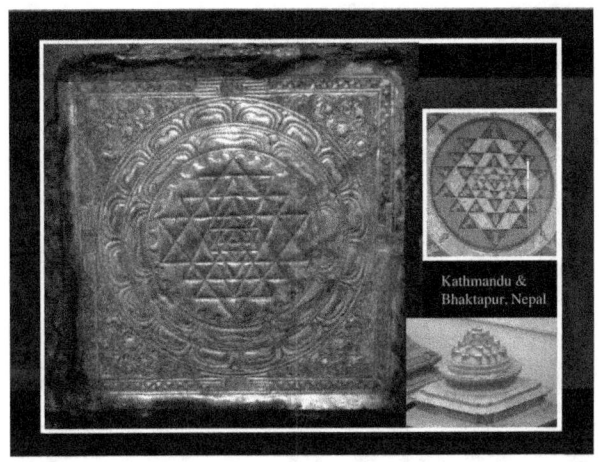

這兩張圖分別來自尼泊爾的加德滿都和巴克塔布林。這張來自巴克塔布林國家博物館。那麼這張圖像的象徵意義就什麼呢？這兩張圖表明，如果我們要看加美穆哈和摩伽羅，我們要直接看進它的嘴裡。如果我們將我們的意識和計畫用到這種認知、渴求、欲望的機制上，那麼這就是我們所看到的。不誇張，而是象徵性地說。研究感知機制時，它只是一個象徵符號。這張圖代表著創造力，慷慨和無窮無盡的富足。

These two images are from Kathmandu and this one here is from Bhaktapur Nepal. It's from the National Museum in Bhaktapur. So what does this image mean? These images represent, if we were to face the kami-mukha or the makara and we were to look directly into its mouth. If we are to take our awareness and project that directly into the mechanism of perception, of desire, of appetite, then this is what we see. Not literally, but symbolically. It's a symbolic representation of looking into the mechanism of perception. And what this image represents is creativity, bountifulness, and fullness without end.

因此，可能又有人會說，"我有欲望，我有需要。"可是如果那人直視需要經驗，那裡沒有需要，只有富足。富足正四面八方地散發開來。現在我們看這張的三維立體圖。這張圖上有一種建築裝飾圖案，讓我們來看看這種圖案。

So, again, a person might say, "I have hunger. I have lack." But if the person looks directly into the experience of lack, there is no lack. There is only fullness. There is fullness radiating outwards in all directions. Here, we see the image in three dimensions. This is an architectural motif that represents the same image. Let's take a look at that.

因此，可能又有人會說，"我有欲望，我有需要。"可是如果那人直視需要經驗，那裡沒有需要，只有富足。富足正四面八方地散發開來。現在我們看這張的三維立體圖。這張圖上有一種建築裝飾圖案，讓我們來看看這種圖案。

This is at a temple complex called Pashupatinath. It's an architectural motif that's the same as the two-dimensional diagrams that we saw. These people here are dropping coins on it for good luck. This architectural motif represents perception, the mechanism of awareness.

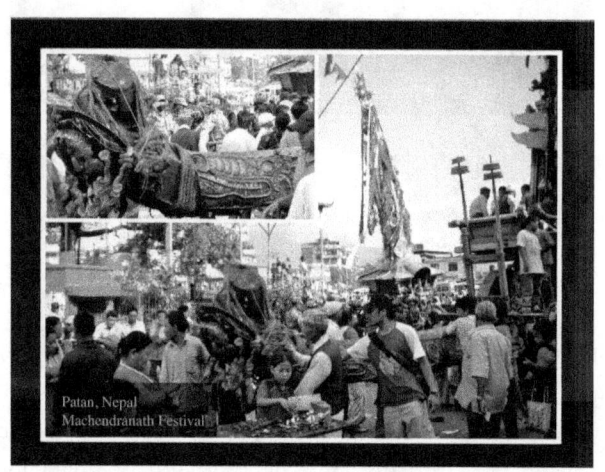

接下來我想向你們展示這張圖，因為我非常喜歡它。這是一張尼泊爾帕坦Matsyendranath節的圖片。Matsyendranath是代表"現在"的神。 由此可見，即使是神性也被理解成一種意識的投影。我們看，這位天神是從摩伽羅的口中出來的，這是心理學層面的東西。這裡有座高約40英尺的塔，人們將它從帕坦的一頭搬到另一頭。這是個盛大的節日。

I just had to show this next image because I love the photograph so much. We are in Patan Nepal during the Matsyendranath Festival. Matsyendranath is this deity represented right here. And what we see is that even a deity is understood as a projection of awareness. We see that the deity is coming out of the makara's mouth. This is very psychological. Here there is a tower that's about forty feet high and people drag it from one end of Patan to the other. It's an amazing festival.

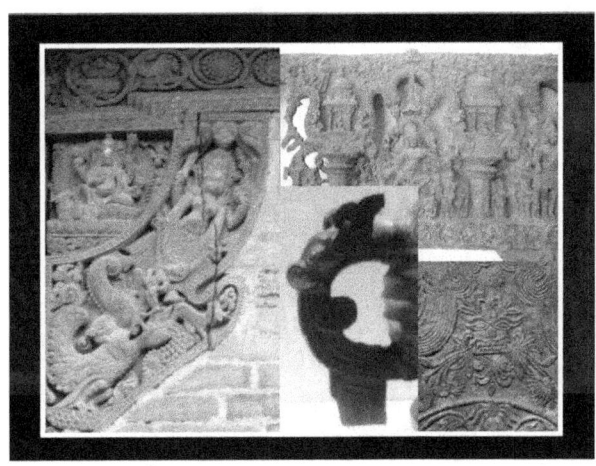

現在我們什麼東西都知道一點了，我們有尼泊爾寺廟兩側的摩伽羅像，我們看到上面有花卉紋，它的嘴裡像流水一樣湧出植物花卉；我們看到動物群，看到一隻鹿從摩伽羅的口中跳出來，我喜歡這只鹿；我們也看到神從摩伽羅的口中跳出來。嘿！印度和尼泊爾的欲望象徵確實非常深奧，而且還含有很多層面的悖論。印度有兩旁繪有摩伽羅的加美穆哈圖；我們看過古西周的把手，此外，液體是從它的嘴裡湧出來的。這正暗示了各種不同的文化思維之間存在著密切的聯繫。不同的人們，不同的文化和不同象徵物的出現，都是以一連串相似的宇宙論和心理學理解為基礎的。佛像之上有形成佛像光暈的那些湧出來的花卉。因此，甚至連佛的大徹大悟也是一種感知機制，當然，這是我們從印度風格中得到的啟示。

Here we have a little bit of everything. We have a makara image on the side of a Nepalese temple. And we see floral motifs in it. There are plants pouring out of its mouth like water. We see fauna, we have a deer that is leaping out of the makara's mouth. I love it. And here we have a goddess who is also leaping out of the makara's mouth. Here, this symbol for appetite is really quite profound in India and Nepal. It has a great deal of paradox. Here in India we have the image of the kami-mukha with the two makaras on either side. Now, here we see the old Zhou dynasty handles. And again, this is liquid pouring out of its mouth. This is very suggestive of a cross-cultural familiarity of ideas, where different people, cultures, and symbols appear to be grounded in familiar threads of cosmological and psychological understandings. Above the Buddha we have this outpouring of flowers that creates the halo of the Buddha. So, even the enlightenment of the Buddha comes from the mechanism of perception, if, of course, we read this from the Indian style.

PART 5:
THE BEAUTY OF THIS PAN-ASIAN
SYMBOL IN CHINESE ARCHITECTURE

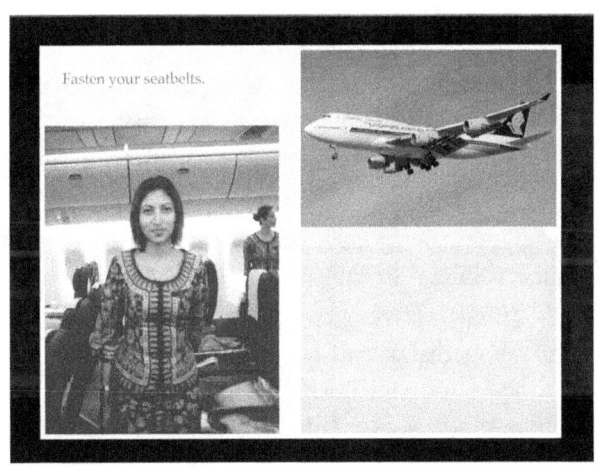

我們透視了各種不同的文化，現在何不系好你的座位安全帶，椅背調到垂直位置，將託盤桌子折疊好呢？祝你們旅途愉快！因為我們要飛回中國。

Now that we have this cross-cultural perspective, why don't we fasten our seatbelts, put your seats in an upright position, secure your tray table, and enjoy your flight, because we are heading back to China.

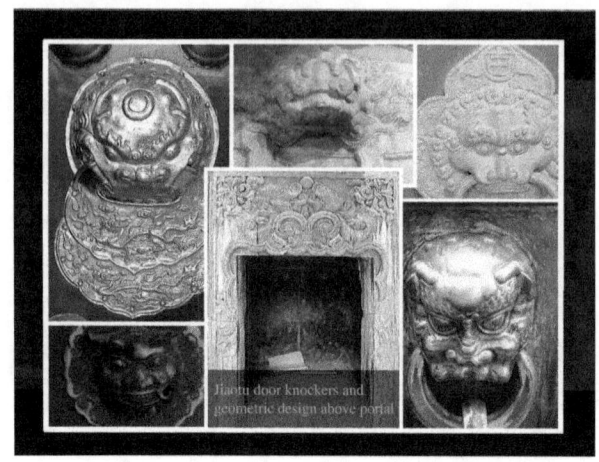

透視了不同的文化，獲得了更廣泛的詞彙，現在我們用這些來檢驗中國的藝術和建築學。讓我們看一些類似的中國圖紋。這裡有個椒圖門環和一個大門上的幾何設計。椒圖也是龍九子之一。我們記得，明朝學者楊慎說饕餮是龍九之一。而椒圖是龍的另外一個兒子。由此可見，甚至連龍的象徵都似乎是從它的口中吐出來的。這讓我們想起，我們最近所看過的圖片。這裡我們有更多圖片。有些看起來非常像獅子。這大門上方的幾何設計可能是狴犴或 xianzhang（龍九子之一），雖然它很幾何圖形化，可是這張圖讓我們想起那張沒有下頷的臉。

With this cross-cultural perspective and with a broader vocabulary with which to examine Chinese art and architecture, let's take a look at some familiar Chinese motifs. Here we have the jiaotu doorknockers and a geometric design above this portal. The jiaotu is another of the nine sons of the dragon. The taotie, we remember, Yang Shen, the Ming dynasty scholar said was one of the nine sons of the dragon. The jiaotu doorknocker is another. So, here we see that even the symbol of the dragon seems to be coming out its mouth. It's very suggestive, given the images that we have recently seen. Here we have some more. Some of them look a lot like a lion. This geometric design above the doorway (perhaps a bi'an or xianzhang) is suggestive of the kami-mukha images above the doorways. And even though it is very geometric, the image is suggestive of a face without a lower jaw.

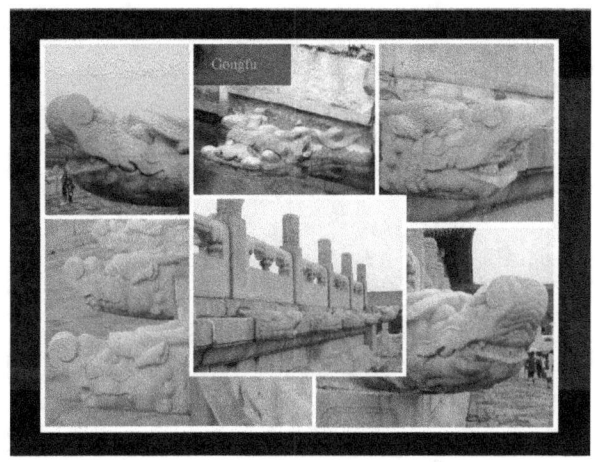

我們這裡有蚣蝮，蚣蝮也是龍九子之一。建築上，它常常用來做排水口。因此，水從它的嘴裡流出來。現在，我們來看看這鼻子。我們之前看過這種鼻子嗎？它的圖案跟有液體從動物口中流出來的周朝手把是一樣的，看上去就像一個噴泉，鼻子是一模一樣的。

Here we have the gongfu. And the gongfu is, again, one of the nine sons of the dragon. Architecturally, it's often used as a waterspout. So, water pours out of its mouth. Now, look at the nose. Have we seen the nose before? It's the same motif as on the Zhou dynasty handles where we see liquid pouring out of the animal's mouth. It looks like a fountain and has the exact same nose.

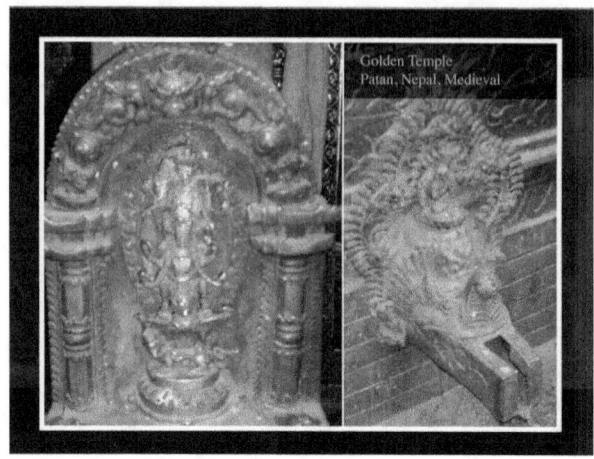

還有，你們記得這個嗎？這個是加美穆哈，還有這個是摩伽羅。嘿！它們有著一樣的鼻子，看上去都非常像蚣蝮圖案中的鼻子。你們怎麼看？這是一種文化傳承？我相信確實如此。

And remember this? This is the kami-mukha and this is the makara. Here, they have the exact same nose, which, again, looks so much like the nose of the gongfu image. What do you think? A cultural continuity? I believe so.

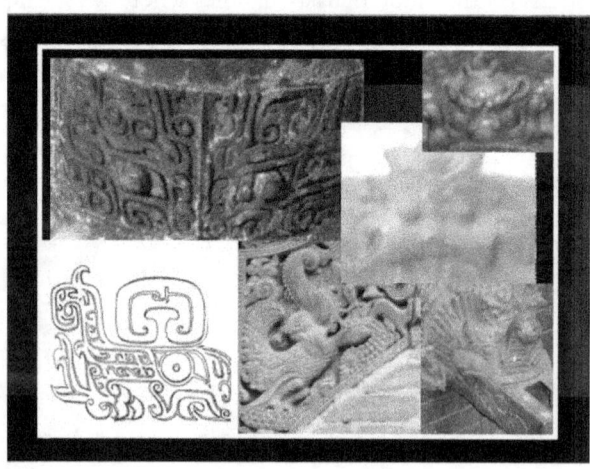

我們這裡，上有饕餮圖，下有側面圖。我們來看看側面圖與摩伽羅有多麼相似！鼻子、爪子、筆直豎在空中的尾部都是如此地相似。這裡有饕餮圖，而這裡有加美穆哈圖。

Here, we have the taotie image at the top, and we have the profile image below. And we see how closely the profile resembles the makara. The snout, the claw, the tail that goes straight up in the air. It's very similar. Here we have the taotie while here we have the kami-mukha.

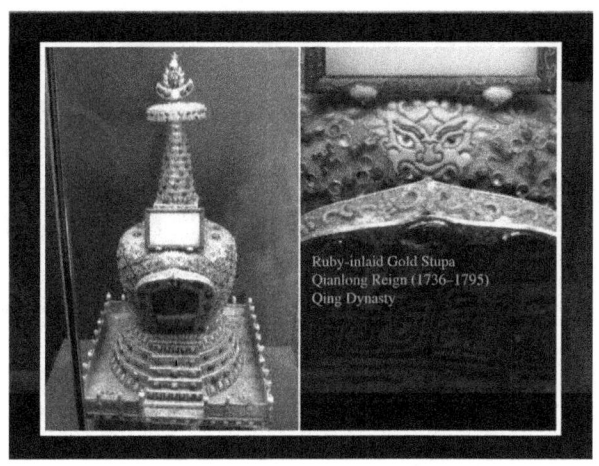

這裡我們有清朝的佛塔，上面有使我們聯想到饕餮的圖紋，還有從它口中湧出來花卉圖案。此外，它也位於門口的上方，就跟我們在印度門口上方看到加美穆哈圖一樣。

Here we have the Qing dynasty stupa with the image that reminds us of the taotie. And it has the floral motif pouring out of its mouth. And again, it is above the doorway, just as we have seen the kami-mukha above the doorways in India.

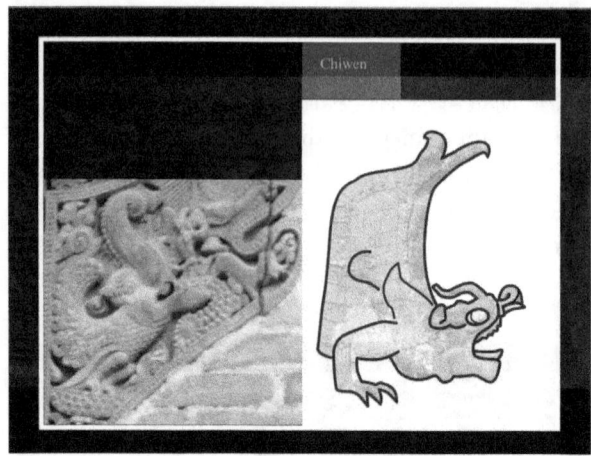

這裡有一種建築裝飾圖案，我們在中國各個朝代都可以看到。它就是螭吻紋。螭吻也是龍九子之一。所以我們看看，它與摩伽羅是多麼的相似：尾巴筆直地豎在空中，鼻子和爪子都非常相似。那麼，我們是在那裡找到這張圖的呢？我們是在哪找到這張代表這種驚人的文化傳承的圖？

Now, there is an architectural motif that we see through most of the dynastic period of China. It's called the chiwen. The chiwen is, again, one of the nine sons of the dragon. So, we see how it resembles the makara: the tail going straight up in the air, the nose, the claws. So, where do we find this image? Where do we find this image that expresses this enormous cultural continuity?

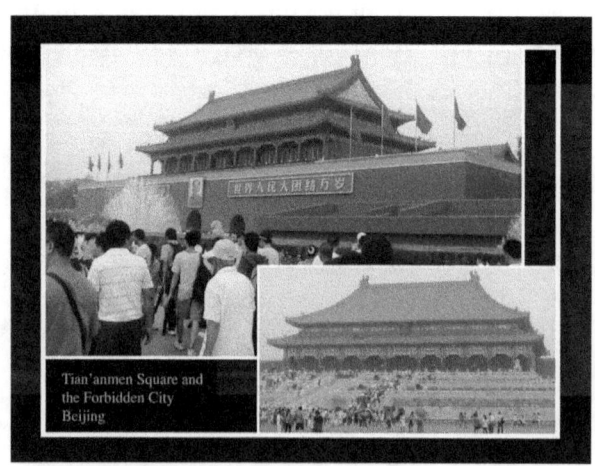

我們是在北京天安門廣場和紫禁城中找到的。為什麼連毛主席像上都有兩張螭吻圖，而且紫禁城的天頂上都有螭吻圖呢？

We find it at Tieniman Square and the Forbidden City in Beijing. Why even above Chairman Mao we have two chiwen images. And in the Forbidden City we have the chiwen images on these rooftops.

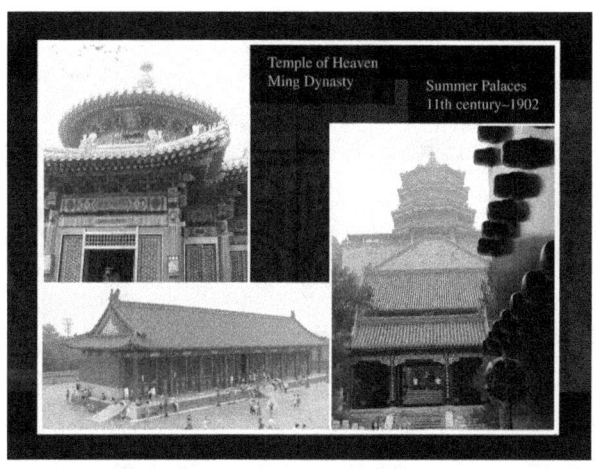

在北京清朝天壇，我們看到螭吻圖，我們能看到它們那筆直豎在空中的尾巴；在頤和園，我們也能看到來自11世紀的螭吻圖。

At the Ming dynasty Temple of Heaven in Beijing, we see the chiwen images. We can see their tails sticking straight up in the air. And here also, at the Summer Palace, which is from the 11th century.

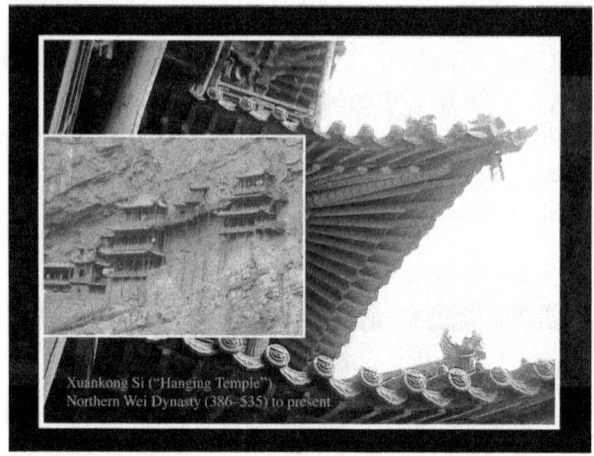

懸空寺從北魏屹立至 今，因為它是建在絕壁上，所以人們必須不
斷地對其修繕，要不然它就會倒塌。那裡我們也看到螭吻圖.

The Hanging Temple, from the northern Wei dynasty to the present.
Because its built on the side of the cliff they have to continually keep
building it, or else it falls. There we see the gongfu image.

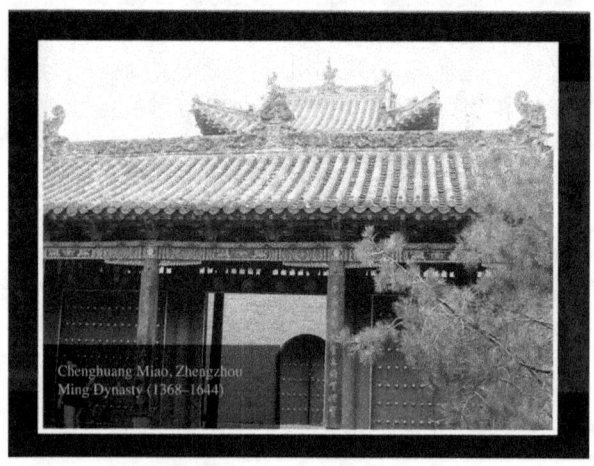

清朝的鄭州城隍廟，我喜歡它的那琉璃瓦做的天頂。那天頂讓人驚
歎不已，這裡我們也能有兩張好看的螭吻圖。

Chenghuang Miao temple in Zhengzhou. This is from the Ming dynasty. I
love the ceramic roof. This is an amazing roof. Here we have two beautiful
chiwen images.

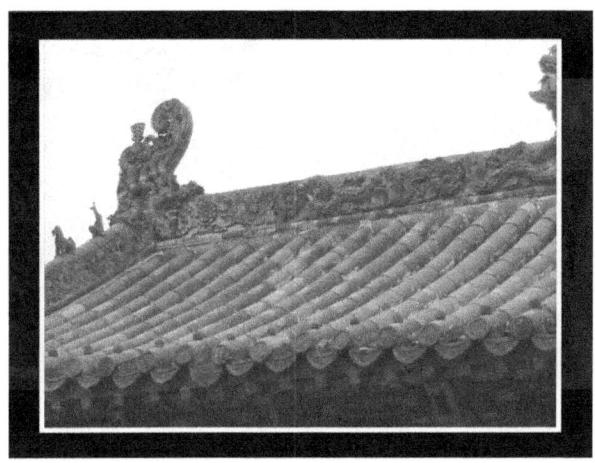

我們看到它們口中湧出來的有花卉圖案和植物形態，樣樣精細入微。螭吻向天頂的對面吐著花卉，而且還往下吐在兩側上。因此兩側的花卉圖案就在中間相接。那麼，讓我們就近看看它們是在中間哪裡相接的。

And we see that pouring out of their mouths are floral motifs, plant forms. There's a lot of detail in these images. The chiwen is pouring flowers out across the rooftop, and its also pouring down the side. So, the floral motifs from both sides meet in the middle. So, let's take a closer look at where they meet in the middle.

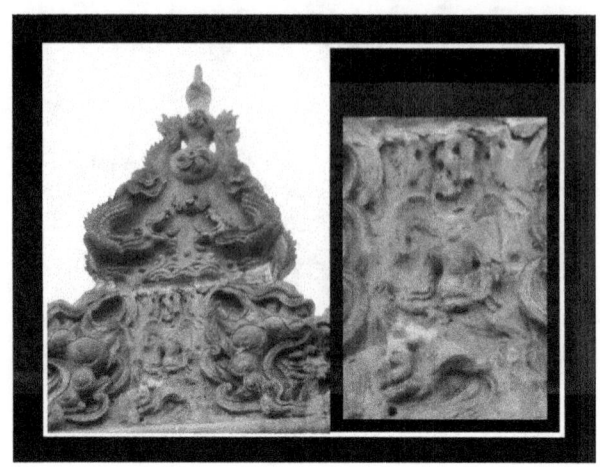

它們就在這裡相接。植物的形態看上去就像水、火或能量。在它們相接的中心位置有個男人。他看上去像一名老師或智者。在他頭頂的上方，我們看到這些象徵性的頭飾或光暈。因此，他肯定是一位很有才華的老師。這張是城隍廟，廟宇不一定是佛教的。它更是各種不同傳統的混合體。它更加融合，代表著多種不同的傳統。

They meet right here. The plant forms almost looks like water, fire, or energy. In the center, where it meets, is a man. He looks like a teacher or a wise man. Above his head we see these symbolic tiaras or halos. So, he must be a very wise teacher. This is at the city god temple. So, the temple is not necessarily Buddhist. It's more a mix of traditions. It's more syncretic, representative of many traditions.

現在我們就近看看這名智者。左下方是他的一名學生。現在我看著這張圖，心裡不禁在想，"我希望能與這人共進午餐。" 那一定是件趣事，我想肯定是一場愉快的交談，對吧？

So here we see a close up of this wise man. And below to the left is one of his students. Now when I see this image, what I say to myself is, "I'd like to have lunch with this guy." That would be fun. I think really good conversation, right?

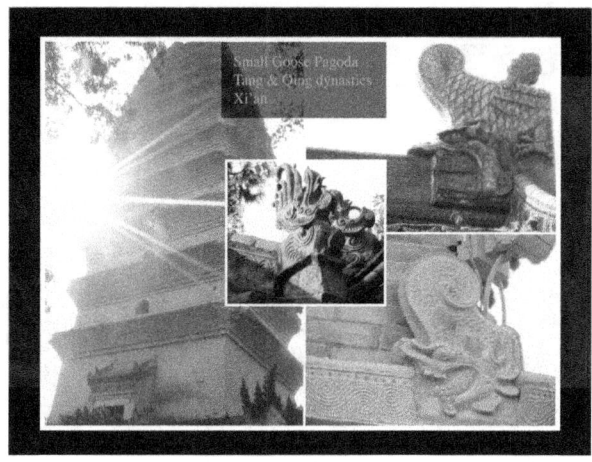

這裡我們來到西安大雁塔，它建於明清時期。因此，這些螭吻可能在近代重新修繕過。能量和水從它們的口中湧出來。我們看，那相似的尾巴也筆直地豎在空中。從螭吻那裡湧出來的能量就灑在這張像龍一樣的圖像上。

Here we are at the Small Goose Pagoda, during the Tang and Qing dynasties, in Xi'an. So, these chiwen might have been rebuilt in the modern period. Energy or water is pouring out of their mouths. We see the familiar tail sticking straight up in the air. The energy pours down from the chiwen and ends in this dragon-like image.

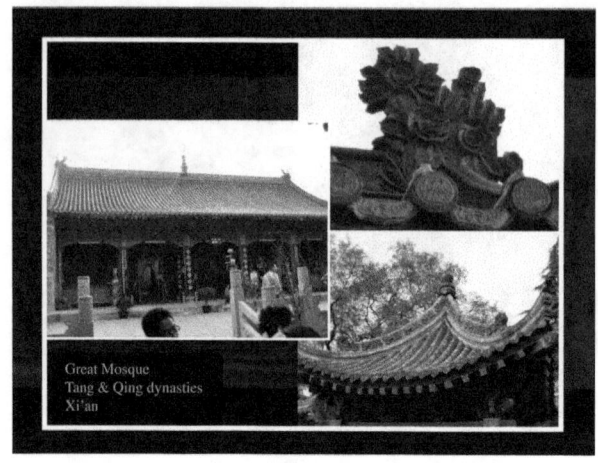

Great Mosque
Tang & Qing dynasties
Xi'an

這是其中最有趣的一頁。我們有建於明清時期的西安清真寺。天頂上的圖案看起來很像螭吻，對嗎？然而，我們單有形式，沒有主體內容。伊斯蘭文化是一種象徵文化，就是說伊斯蘭文化不像複製人物或動物圖那樣，肯定也不會複製怪獸圖。因此，它上面是一束花，而不是螭吻紋；它上面沒有一幅暗示渴求和欲望的怪獸圖，而是一束花。沒有任何象徵性符號。

This is one of the most interesting pages. We have the Great Mosque in Xi'an from the Tang and Qing dynasties. That looks like the chiwen on the rooftop, right? However, we have the form but none of the content. Islamic culture is aniconic. Which means that Islamic culture does not like to reproduce images of people or animals. And certainly not monsters. So, instead of a chiwen is a bouquet of flowers. Instead of the monster image, an image suggestive of hunger, of appetite, we get a bouquet flowers. None of the symbolic content whatsoever.

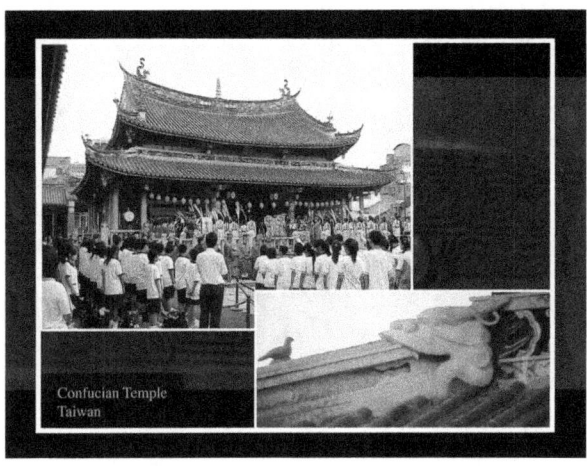

在臺灣省的夫子廟裡，我們看到蚣蝮圖。那種建築樣式本身就是從它的口中吐出來的。你們看這些鳥類的形態，是貓頭鷹---象徵著儒家文化甚至對那些反叛學生的大度包容。貓頭鷹被視為不祥之鳥。現在來看天頂，那裡的螭吻很像龍。真有趣極了！

In Taiwan, at a Confucian temple we have the gongfu image. The architecture itself is pouring out of its mouth. Look at these bird forms. They're owls, a Confucian symbol for how Confucius' teachings are accessible even to aggressive students. The owl being thought of as a troublesome bird. Now, on the rooftop, the chiwen resembles a dragon. That's interesting.

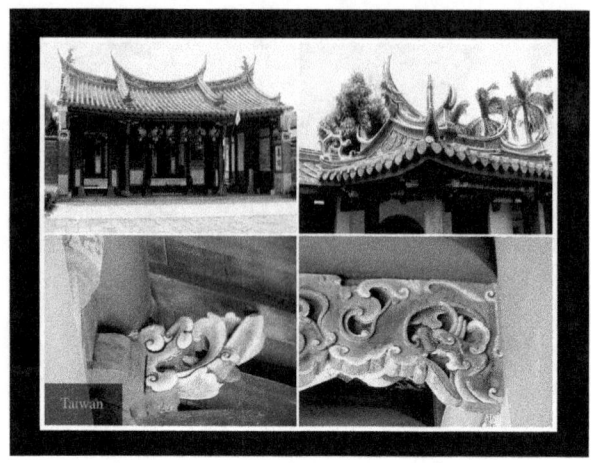

這裡有些臺灣省的廟宇。這張螭吻也跟龍像極了，不過我們仍能認出它是常見的螭吻。這廟裡同樣有蚣蝮，它看起來也像一條龍。這裡的兩邊，我們發現這些看上去像蚣蝮但也象龍的建築元素。這兩張圖看起來也像一種轉化的狀態。它們看上去像一種演變的狀態：由一種東西轉變成為另一種東西的過程。這就是中國文化的中心思想。我想起易經或太極圖，陰可以轉化成陽。同樣地，蚣蝮圖看上去好像正轉化成雲或者水，或者是龍，又或者是花，對嗎？誰知道呢！它看上去好像正處於轉化的中途。還有這張，它是一條龍、一條蚣蝮還是波浪呢？

Here are some more temples in Taiwan province. This chiwen also strongly resembles a dragon, but still we can see that it is the familiar chiwen. This temple also has a gongfu, which also looks like a dragon. Here, on the sides, we see these architectural elements which look like the gongfu, but they also resemble dragons. These two images also look like a state of transformation. They look like a state of flux. One thing transforming into another. Now, this is a central idea in Chinese culture. I think of the I Ching or the taijitu diagram. Yin turns to yang. And similarly here, the gongfu image looks like its turning into clouds, or water, or a dragon, or flowers, right? Who knows? It looks like it's in the middle of transformation. And this one here, is this a dragon, a gongfu, or waves?

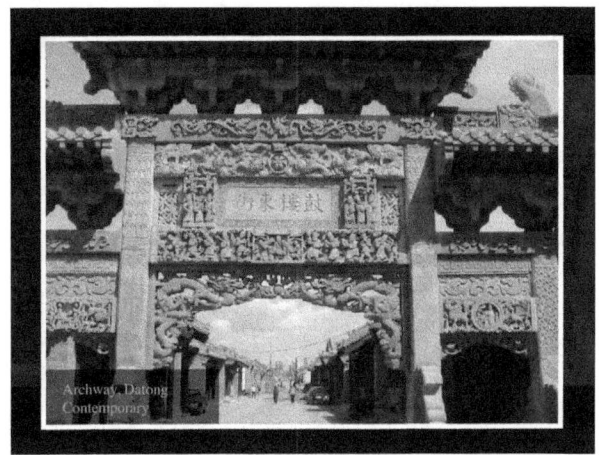

這裡我們有一道拱形門廊。這是當代的建築物，是新建的。我去大同時，他們正在興建這道拱門。天頂處，我們看見了螭吻圖。這裡，我們看到兩張蚣蝮圖。它們當中，是一張像饕餮的圖，它看上去真的很像加美穆哈。不是嗎？我想跟設計此圖的建築師或 雕刻家談談，因為他們對這些風格必定有很深的研究。多麼好的一幅作品啊！

Here we have an archway in Datong. This is contemporary. This is new. When I went to Datong they were building this. On the rooftop we see the chiwen images. Here, we see two gongfu images. In the center of them is a taotie-like image that really resembles the kami-mukha. Doesn't it? I'd like to talk to the architect or the sculptor who designed this because they must have studied these forms a lot. What a nice piece of work.

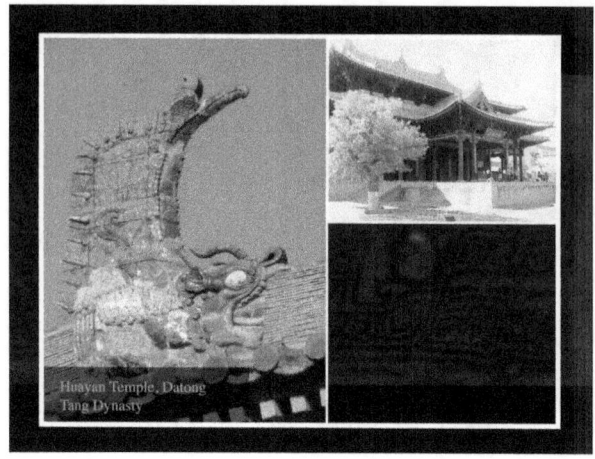

這裡是大同華嚴寺，建於唐朝年間。你們看這些瓷磚，這是我最喜歡的圖形之一。多漂亮啊！光滑的綠瓷製品多麼的引人注目啊，還有那是寺廟的天頂。

Here is the Huayan temple in Datong, built during the Tang dynasty. Look at the ceramic tiles. This is one of my favorite images. Isn't that beautiful. The glazed green ceramic work is outstanding. And there it is on the rooftop of the temple.

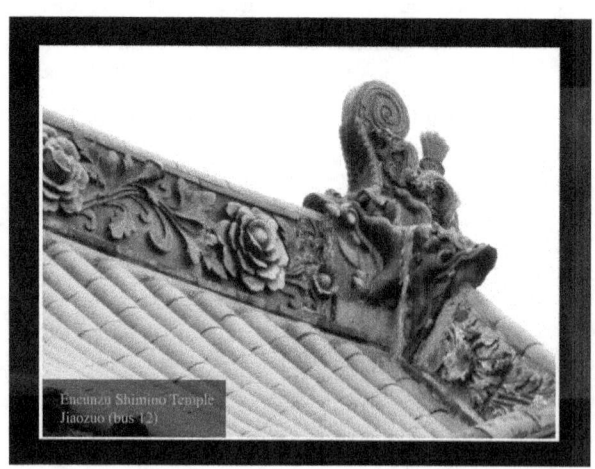

這裡是焦作的恩村祖師廟。你們看這些陶瓷製品多漂亮啊。難道不引人注目嗎？這裡我們又看到椒圖像了。我們看那此花卉紋。

And here we have the Encunzu Shimino temple in Jiaozuo. Look at how beautiful the ceramic work is. Isn't this outstanding? Here we have the jiaotu image again. And we see the the floral motif.

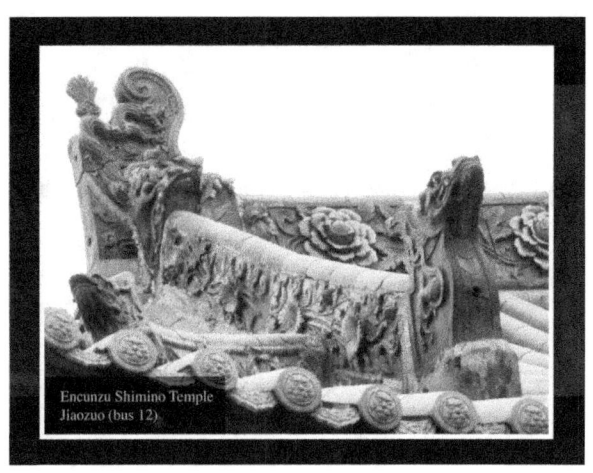

花卉從它口中吐出，湧向天頂對面，還從天頂向下流。多像從它口中湧出來的花河和能量河啊。河流在一條小溪那裡中斷了。河流跟小流一起向那些像龍一樣的圖像湧過去。

Flowers are pouring out of its mouth across the roof, and also down the roof. It's like a river of flowers and energy pouring out of its mouth. And a stream breaks off from this river. The river and stream both end in these dragon-like images.

THE TAOTIE IMAGE IN CHINESE ART, CULTURE, AND COSMOLOGY

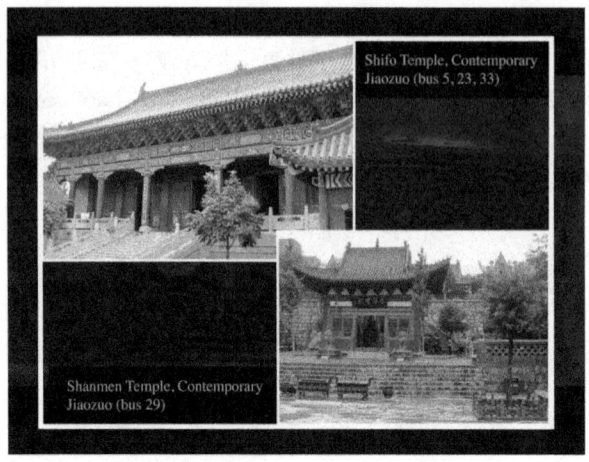

Shifo Temple, Contemporary
Jiaozuo (bus 5, 23, 33)

Shanmen Temple, Contemporary
Jiaozuo (bus 29)

當代的山門寺是新建的。如果你曾爬過針尖山，這寺廟就在山的背後，在那裡，你能看見這些天頂上的螭吻圖。在焦作，我相信你可以乘坐29路和37路公車到達那裡。

Shanmen temple, contemporary. This is new. If you've ever been to needle mountain you have this temple behind the mountain, where you can see these chiwen images on the rooftops. In Jiaozuo you can reach this temple by bus 29 and also 37, I believe.

這裡是當代建築石佛寺。我去那裡時，人們正在修建此寺。你在那裡可以看到天頂上漂亮的螭吻。在焦作，你可以乘坐5路、23路或37路公車到達那裡。

Here we have the Shifo temple. This is contemporary. When I went there, people were building this. You can see the nice chiwen on the rooftop. In Jiaozuo you can get to this temple by bus 5, 23, or 33.

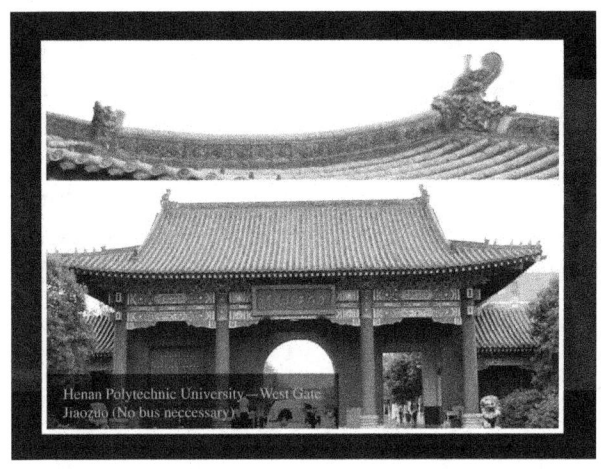

焦作河南理工大學西門　你們不需要坐車，它就在這裡。

Henan Polytechnic University, West Gate. Jiaozuo. No bus necessary. That's right here.

天頂上有螭吻。相當好看。那邊有兩條螭吻，嘴裡湧出水、能量或花卉。能量從側邊向下流入一條河裡，再次在一條小溪那裡中斷。因此，你去到西門，看著天頂處的螭吻時，你是在看著獨特的文化連續性。你是在看一種可以輕易追溯到商朝青銅圖片的連續性。你是在看一種泛亞文化的連續性，一種發展到印度、尼泊爾，甚至泰國去的文化連續性。你也是在看一種最可能表達舊石器時代世界觀的文化連續性。此外，它還是一種從西班牙延續到韓國的文化風格。這是歐亞人類歷史上持續最久的文化風格。所以，當你望向天頂時，你正看著奇妙的文化連續性。

So, there is the chiwen on the rooftop. Quite beautiful. There are two chiwen with water, energy, or flowers pouring out of their mouths. The energy flows down the side in a river, which again, breaks off in a stream. So when you go to the West Gate and you look at the chiwen on the rooftop, you are looking at an extraordinary continuity of culture. You're looking at a continuity that easily extends back to the Shang dynasty bronze images. You're looking at a continuity of culture that is pan-Asian. It's a continuity of culture that extends into India, Nepal, even Thailand. You're also looking at a continuity of culture that most likely expresses a worldview of the Paleolithic. And this is a cultural style that, again, extended from Spain to Korea. It is the longest sustained cultural-style in Eurasian human history. So, when you look at the roofs, you are looking at a tremendous cultural continuity.

我以譚盾的音樂作為本演講的開頭，所以，你會記得譚盾曾說過，關於他的音樂，他要將殷商編鐘融入這首交響曲中，對他來說，這些殷商編鐘代表著未來。

I began this lecture with music from Tan Dun. So, you'll remember that Tan dun had said, regarding his music, that he needed to use Shang dynasty bronze bells in this symphony. And that, for him, these Shang dynasty bronze bells represent the future.

［播放音樂］
[music plays.]

《未來》
The future.

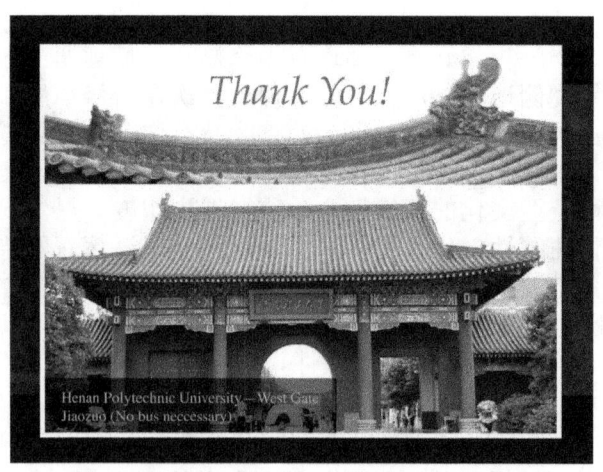

非常感謝！
Thank you very much.

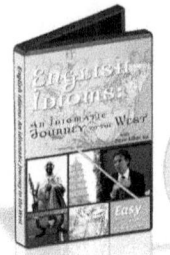
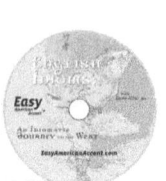

English Idioms: An Idiomatic Journey to the West™ CreateSpace (2013)

English Idioms: An Idiomatic Journey to the West is a DVD to learn American English.

> "I really enjoyed your lecture. I think this lecture is of great help to me. I like your lecture style and the very lively humor. There was a lot of student interaction time. The most important thing for me is making learning fun."
>
> **Zheng Yingchao (Betty),**
> University Student at *English Idioms* lecture

Part 1: What Are Idioms?

You'll learn, "What are Idioms?"

- First, you'll focus on the dictionary definition and word origin of idiom.

- Second, you'll understand idiomatic expressions as English grammar. Idioms often use figurative language: metaphor, simile, personification, onomatopoeia, and oxymoron.

- You'll examine the sentence structure of English idioms, slang, phrases, and figures of speech.

- Finally, you'll learn how language is culture.

> "Firstly, I thank you for giving us a wonderful presentation. It helped me in English idioms. I learned a lot from it. The performance was also wonderful. I liked it very much. Your spoken English is very pleasant to listen to. I got lots from the presentation. I know that English is also amusing. It gave me confidence to practice and I believe I can do it!"
>
> **Zhu Xin,**
> University Student at *English Idioms* lecture

Part 2: An Idiomatic Journey to the West

Idioms are used to explain *The Journey to the West*, a Classical Chinese adventure.

This popular Chinese Ming dynasty book, tells the story of a Tang dynasty monk who travels to India in search of Buddhist scriptures. In Chinese legend, this monk, Xuanzang, meets Sun Wukong, the monkey king.

- You'll learn the meaning of animal idioms, such as, "monkey around," and "pig sty."

- Piggy, Sandy, and the white horse also travel west in this classical Chinese myth.

- Guan Yin even makes an appearance in the story (and English class) before the end of the journey at Xi'an.

> "From this lecture, I learned idioms and knowledge. It makes me know that English and Chinese actually are extensive and profound."
>
> **Luo Zhen,**
> University Student at *English Idioms* lecture

In this idiomatic *Journey to the West* movie . . .

- you'll learn American pronunciation from the English coach and trainer, Dave Alber.

- You'll get practical English training practicing sentences with idioms.

- You'll learn new English vocabulary and English phrases.

- You'll get the meaning and definition of a phrase. Often, an idiom's definition or the meaning of a phrase includes an explanation of American slang.

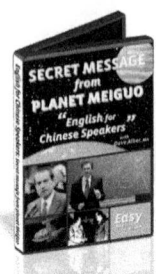
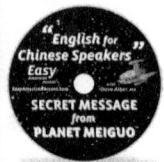

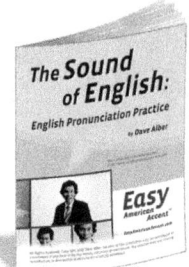

The Sound of English: English Pronunciation Practice™
CreateSpace (2013)

This book teaches English pronunciation.

The Sound of English: English Pronunciation Practice is an English training book that focuses on *speaking English* and the *sounds of English pronunciation*.

English sounds and pronunciation are essential in order to speak good English. Therefore, when people want to learn English, they need to focus on how to speak English. Because English is a phonetic language, spoken English is vital for learning English. This is a key point, English pronunciation is essential for clear speech. You can communicate with confidence and clearly express your ideas only after you gain the knowledge of the sound of the English language.

The Sound of English: English Pronunciation Practice:

- organizes the *vowel sounds* in an easy to use table. This table is great for pronunciation drills.

- Next, the *consonant sounds* are described and presented in many practical examples.

- **The Sound of English** describes how to make the *English vowel and consonant sounds*. Then shows how they are used in the beginning, middle, and end of words.

- Finally, *consonant clusters* are given in a table, so that you can practice each consonant cluster in many examples. You receive fun practice paragraphs, for the vowels and consonants, that will soon have you speaking English like a native speaker.

If you, or someone you know, recognizes the rewards of speaking English clearly, then *The Sound of English: English Pronunciation Practice* is the confident choice.

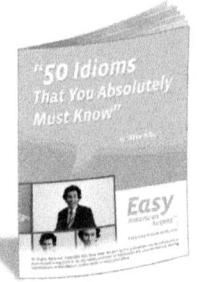

50 Idioms That You Absolutely Must Know ™
CreateSpace (2013)

This book teaches American English idioms.

Idioms That You Absolutely Must Know teaches essential idioms. These *English idioms* are both American and English idioms. The dictionary definition and meaning of these *idiomatic expressions* is presented. Then the English idiom is used in an example. Lots of American slang, American phrases, proverbs, and figures of speech come alive through the brief examples. Examples are useful in business English or regular American life. This short book is written by Dave Alber, English teacher, English pronunciation trainer, Principle at EasyAmericanAccent.com, and creator of *English Idioms: An Idiomatic Journey to the West* and *English For Chinese Speakers: Secret Message From Planet Meiguo.*

For a **LIMITED TIME** this book, and a **special audio version of this book** will be available for **FREE** when you purchase *English Idioms: An Idiomatic Journey to the West* online from the www.**easyamericanaccent.com** website.

ABOUT THE AUTHOR

Dave Alber, MA is an enthusiastic Religious Studies lecturer
and English Teacher who has taught English at the university level
in China and the Middle East. He comes from a Quaker Protestant
background, has an MA in Mythological Studies, and extensive immersion
in Asian religious traditions. His global exposure to the religious life on four
continents gives him the ability to lecture from direct experience on a
variety of religious traditions: whether festivals in America, Asia, or Africa;
Koranic doctrine in Arabic culture; meditation in the style of Ethiopian
Coptic Christians, Indian Hindus, or Buddhists.

He is also the Principal at http://www.easyamericanaccent.com and the
author of *"50 Idioms That You Absolutely Must Know"* and *The Sound of English:
English Pronunciation Practice*, amongst other books. His DVDs include
English Idioms: An Idiomatic Journey to the West and *Secret Message From
Planet Meiguo: English for Chinese Speakers*.

He is available as a Religious Studies lecturer and English Teacher and
trainer or pronunciation and American accent consultant.

关于作者

戴夫・阿爾伯文學碩士是狂熱的宗教研究講師，也是一位在中國和
中東大學執教的英語教師。他有基督新教貴格會的背境，取得了神
話研究碩士學位，對宗教傳統有很深的研究。四大洲的宗教生活的
全球接觸，多種多樣宗教傳統的親身體驗，賦予了他出色的演講能
力：無論是美國和亞洲的節日，還是阿拉伯中的可蘭經和教義、埃
塞俄比亞科普特基督教徒風格的冥想、印度教徒或佛教徒等等。
他目前在潛心鑽研比較宇宙學。
此外，他還是http://www.easyamericanaccent.com的校長和《你
必須瞭解的50個習慣用語》作者，除了其他書之外，他還著有另外
一本書《英語之聲：英語發音練習》。他的DVD包括英語習慣用語
《習慣用語西遊記》和適合中國人學發音的《來自美國星球的機密》
他既是一名宗教研究講師，還是英語教師、教練或發音指導和美
國口音顧問。